# The Trans-Cultural Study Guide

By Volunteers in Asia

Second Edition

Edited by

Kenneth Darrow
Bradley Palmquist

## CREDITS

| | |
|---|---|
| *Cover:* | Winnie Lum |
| *Chinese Calligraphy:* | Prof. Kai-yu Hsu |
| *Cartoons (pp. 27,33,46):* | Paula, reprinted from CERES, the FAO review |
| *Book Design:* | Ken Darrow |
| *Typography:* | Pacifica Services, Palo Alto, Calif. |

# Contents

# Foreword

*The making of this guide has truly been a group effort. All of us who have contributed have in some way been involved with Volunteers in Asia--a small, people-oriented group based in Stanford, California, that provides volunteer work and study opportunities in Asia. From the beginning, VIA's emphasis has been on increasing understanding between cultures. This guide is both a part of that endeavor, and a reflection of it.*

*Why the Study Guide? Because we believe that direct observation and participation, when complemented by systematic inquiry, can lead to a clearer perception of another culture and people. We believe that the questions one asks determine to a large extent the answers and conclusions that follow. We have tried to direct the questions in this guide from a humanitarian perspective.*

*Although this guide, written by Americans, reflects to some degree the culture of those who produced it, it was designed to facilitate inquiry into any country or culture, by students anywhere. It has been helpful to American students and volunteers living in different countries. Hopefully, it can be used as a tool for other nationals in crossing cultural boundaries.*

*Two individuals deserve special mention here. One is Dan Morrow, who originally conceived of the idea of a series of questions grouped into topic areas, to be used by volunteers in the field. This led to the first study guide, which appeared in 1972, edited by Dan and Grey Bryan. The second individual is Dwight Clark, whose great enthusiasm, undaunted spirit, and seemingly limitless energy have been vital to Volunteers in Asia the past thirteen years. This study guide draws on the exper-*

*iences of more than a dozen VIA volunteers who were able to live, work, and study in Asia due in large part to Dwight's efforts.*

*This second edition, much larger than the first, is thoroughly revised, incorporating continued input from a number of returned volunteers. Besides adding more than half a dozen new sections, we have made numerous changes in content and format. Short quotations have been included from a variety of sources. These, we feel, contain important and provocative ideas to be grappled with. They reflect differing viewpoints and merit thoughtful reactions.*

*In writing the Study Guide, we have tried to be aware of our remaining ethnocentrism and the need to be more sensitive to those with whom we live, work, and study. We hope that the reader will affirm the inherent value and integrity of each culture as an expression of mankind's diversity and potential. We look towards a time of global community when decisions will be based upon mutual interests, respect, and understanding.*

*Portions of this guide were written by Grey Bryan, Ken Darrow, Seth Greenberg, Susan Martin, Shelley Metzenbaum, Mary Michael McTeague, Dan Morrow, Brad Palmquist, Rich Rawson, Maya and Nick Selby, and Scott Silverman. A special thanks to Phil Mease for providing us with excellent material for the section on Health.*

*--Kenneth Darrow*
*Bradley Palmquist*
*1975 Editors*

# Introduction

Whoever is spared personal pain
must feel himself called to help in
diminishing the pain of others. We must
all carry our share of the misery
which lies upon the world.

—Albert Schweitzer

If a knew for a certainty that a man
was coming to my house with the conscious design of doing me good, I should
run for my life...for fear that I should get
some of his good done to me...A man is
not a good man to me because he will
feed me if I should be starving, or warm
me if I should be freezing, or pull me out
of a ditch if I should ever fall into one.
I can find you a Newfoundland
dog that will do as much.

—Henry Thoreau

# Introduction

*'Men, even good men, are commonly disposed to submit to the slavery of the actual; they literally cannot imagine themselves in any life situation other than the one in which they live.'*

**—Daniel Berrigan**

This book has been written to stimulate the imagination. To make other life-ways more comprehensible. That is our hope.

Is it really true that all people are brothers and sisters? We think so. We all laugh and we all cry; we all have our dreams and our disappointments.

Yet this ancient idea, as old as mankind--appearing in some form in all the world's religions, and written into the charter of every international organization--is often pushed aside and forgotten in times of crisis.

It seems that we lack a certain solid familiarity with the ways and dreams of other peoples. The smiles of children in another land kindle a warmth within us that can bring us to the point of almost really understanding that word, brotherhood. Yet this warmth is quickly dissipated by the cold steel of wartime, by the military solution. How soon we forget!

But can we really expect to embrace the unfamiliar on faith alone, without real understanding? Our friends and those we love and hold dear, by and large are not rice farmers. So long as we cannot begin to imagine life as a rice farmer, we cannot fully understand and live out the idea (with all its implications) that all humans comprise one humanity. Brotherhood remains an abstraction too large to comprehend, too vague to act upon decisively, too intangible to make sacrifices for, too distant for the effects to be seen. The fears that motivate the military solution will continue to obscure the warmth of brotherhood.

A need for compassionate understanding is what

concerns those who put together this book. It is designed to be a guide to study, observation, inquiry, and contemplation. We hope it will help lead to a more thorough examination of another society, of another people, of another way.

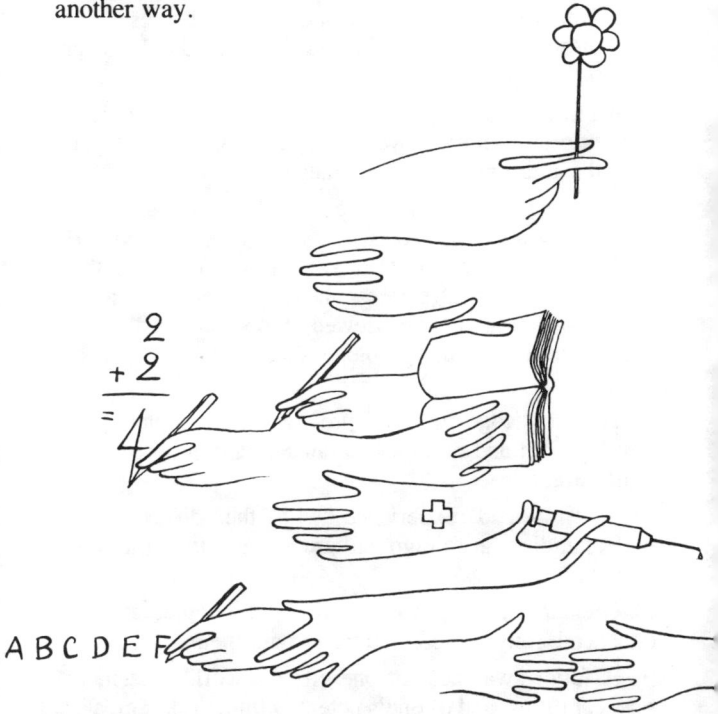

## A. Learning Goals

This study guide has been designed with the following learning goals in mind:

1) A knowledge and understanding of the country in which one is living as a foreigner, including an appreciation of its recent historical experience.

2) A greater understanding of the process and problems of cross-cultural and international contact on both the personal level and the national level.

3) An appreciation of the way in which this country views the rest of the world; its international interests; and how these interests are perceived and reacted to by other nations.

4) An awareness of the overseas interests and activities of your own country, how these affect other peoples, and how these are perceived by other peoples.

5) A clearer understanding of foreign assistance programs, and the roles of foreigners as tourists, students, and commercial or service workers; how this foreign presence affects the host country; how these people and programs are viewed by both the 'hosts' and the 'visitors'; and the problems that arise from each of these.

6) A knowledge of the process and problems of development and rapid social change, and prospects for the future.

7) A first-hand experience with the difficulty of understanding a foreign culture in all its depth and diversity.

8) Greater empathy with a different people, and an enhanced ability to communicate with them.

9) A fuller awareness of oneself as a world citizen, of one's abilities, and of one's potential future roles; greater confidence, direction, and commitment.

10) A new perspective on one's native land upon return from abroad.

## B. Using the Study Guide

You will not be able to explore all of the areas outlined in the study guide; however, we hope that the categories and questions will be a guide for both a comprehensive overview and a detailed study of one or more particular areas. It must be emphasized that the topic areas of the study guide represent artificial divisions. Any serious inquiry into a particular problem will lead the reader across topic areas (e.g. the world food crisis as it appears in any country can be systematically examined with the help of portions of the economics (agriculture, international trade), health (nutrition, family planning), social structure, and politics sections).

---

**Helper/helpee relationships are vitiated by a structural paternalism which impedes growth for both partners. Every master is a slave and every exploiter himself is an exploited man. Except where genuine reciprocity can be established in relationships, these lead to manipulation on the one hand, servility on the other.**

**--Denis Goulet**

---

The questions are designed to be general rather than specific for each country, and to provide adequate flexibility to meet a wide variety of possible situations in the host culture. Many of the questions can be easily broken down into several, more specific questions. We have tried to phrase questions from a variety of viewpoints. Nevertheless, our questions are clearly suggestive rather than definitive. They stress the importance of detailed observation of immediate circumstances as well as the need for generalized observations and theories. They are a guide to what the student should try to learn and also a constant reminder of how much he does not yet know.

Preparation before departure will be essential if the study guide is to be of maximum benefit. You should do background reading on the history, politics, economics, and culture of the country in which you will live.

Before departure, you should review the study guide thoroughly, to familiarize yourself with its form and content. If you will be doing a research project, you should select one or two topic areas of special interest, and begin planning the project. However, it may be that new interests will develop while you are abroad, and opportunities for new projects will present themselves. Be conscious that your research methodology itself, as developed prior to actual contact with the particular culture under study, may be inappropriate and need to be revised or discarded altogether.

While abroad, you can turn to many sources for information. Sources will include available books, magazines, newspapers, and other printed materials, data from government agencies, discussions with friends and students, somewhat formal interviews, informal surveys, direct observation, and introspection. You must always ask questions of yourself and others and seek out new sources of information. (see *Methodology*)

Avoid the pitfall of equating *traditional* with *static*, or even, in many cases, *indigenous*. For the most part, socio-cultural entities have always been undergoing change. Before the era of colonialism and especially modern communications, this change tended to be primarily an internal dynamic. The spread of ideas through external culture contact has always been an important force in this process, but until relatively recently in the history of man, a culture was in a certain sense able to choose among these ideas, and reinterpret them. This maintained the integrity of the socio-cultural entity.

With the advent of the modern era of communications-particularly the widespread distribution of motion pictures and radio--contact between cultures has accelerated tremendously. Even in remote peasant villages, numerous so-called *modern* ideas and material goods are to be found. Hence the terms *traditional*, and *indigenous*, as well as *modern, western*, and numerous others found throughout this guide, must be used carefully, with a full understanding of their limitations.

## C. Living Sensitively in Another Culture

Living sensitively in a culture different from your own is not made easy simply through good intentions. Two areas of special concern are the different styles of non-verbal communication (including such things as gestures, expressions, voice quality, and posture); and the different expectations for behavior and rules of etiquette that you will find.

The following ideas should prove helpful:

1) What to you is quite innocuous may communicate something entirely different in the new cultural context, *and* vice versa. You may not understand messages that are obvious to the local people. Similarly, the non-verbal cues you give spontaneously and naturally may be misinterpreted.

2) Expectations of you can be very difficult to predict and place in their proper context. At times, you will be expected to behave in the same ways as the local people, even though these ways may be quite foreign to you. Many people are unaware of their own ethnocentrism with respect to foreigners. At other times, stricter expectations may be made of you, that do not apply to local people. And on still other occasions, you may find rules of etiquette lifted for you for any number of reasons (which may include an appreciation of the difficulty of your position as a foreigner; tolerance; or special respect).

3) Sometimes local people may act towards you in ways that are actually unacceptable by their own cultural standards. This could be because the standards do not apply in these instances, or because the local people assume that you don't know or don't care; or it could be for other reasons entirely.

4) Every culture has a wide variety of individuals and a correspondingly wide variety of individual behaviors. Most of them fall into categories that are socially defined

as acceptable, but some do not. And even those that do often depend on the context and the persons involved.

In the light of the above suggestions, the importance of being sensitive to local unwritten rules clearly cannot be overemphasized. You cannot always be certain of exactly what is being communicated, or what is expected of you. Be wary of judgements you make of other people based on assumed intentions or meanings, and be careful of extrapolating acceptable behavior solely on the basis of actions you observe. Close friends can often be of help in clarifying what is appropriate in different situations.

You obviously can't continue to live as you did in your own culture. On the other hand, it is quite probably not acceptable for you to live exactly as the local people do. You will have to discover your own middle ground.

Most likely there will be rules or expectations that will be difficult to follow or fulfill. At times you may choose not to. Here again, the implications of your decisions will probably not be immediately apparent. At such times, it is best to know in advance what reactions are likely to be forthcoming, and how you will affect others. A balance needs to be found between maintaining your own sense of self and avoiding *cultural imperialism*. Many aspects of yourself that at first seem essential, may in time seem unnecessary or disadvantageous *cultural baggage*.

# Methodology

If we begin with certainties,
we shall end in doubt;
but if we begin with doubts,
and are patient with them,
we shall end in certainties.

—Francis Bacon

# Methodology

The following list of suggestions is designed to facilitate your work of finding, organizing, and recording data of various kinds. For the most part, these are very practical suggestions and not methodological theory or techniques. We feel, however, that for one who lacks field experience of any kind, even the simplest suggestions may prove to be helpful.

## Finding Books and Printed Material

You will be able to take a few books with you which may be of use in your studies of the country; select these carefully. For the most part, however, you will have to find books there, and the libraries to which you are accustomed may be few and far between. We suggest the following:

1) There may be local libraries, especially those within the universities or colleges, which have useful books, especially about national history or current problems. Ask for permission to use such libraries and check them thoroughly soon after your arrival.

2) You will probably have several friends, especially older people such as professors, who have collections of books. Mention to them that you are looking for books on a particular subject and ask if they know where you might find them. If they have such books, they will probably not hesitate to loan them to you (assuming that you will return them promptly); if they don't, they may know someone who does. Also, your own students (if you are teaching) may have books you could borrow.

3) Local and national newspapers, some of which are in English, may be an invaluable source of information. Not only should you read them daily but also you should try to have a copy from which you can clip articles regularly. Clipping papers is much faster than making

notes and will provide you with a great deal of data by the end of your stay. Articles should be carefully dated and could be organized according to topic by the numbers of the questions from this booklet. You may also want to attach comments or cross-references to an article. Clippings could be kept in folders or a small box.

4) There may be bookstores in the area which, if nothing else, may contain information booklets printed by the government. Browse through any such stores as soon as you have a chance.

5) Offices of government ministries or bureaus may have printed material available, such as census data, policy statements, regulations, or brochures. As long as the information is not at all sensitive and as long as you introduce and explain yourself and your interest thoroughly, you may be able to copy or borrow such material. Ask friends for introductions into these government offices if possible. This would be especially feasible for studies of public health or education.

## Conversations and Interviews

It would obviously be a tragic loss of opportunity to spend most of your time reading. Most of your knowledge about your setting will come through your daily contacts with students and friends, and through special trips or meetings. In many ways, you will employ the methodology of the ethnographer, who learns about a culture primarily as a participant-observor and also through an in-depth knowledge of a few, carefully chosen persons (informants). Here are a few suggestions:

1) Always carry a pocket notebook with you. On any one day, you can pick up many bits of information, usually through conversations, or make new observations. You should make memory-jogging notes as soon as possible so that you can later record and elaborate from these notes. In order to make notes during a conversation without making anyone uncomfortable,

you can, by explaining that you are trying to learn the language, ask about and write down key words. (You should have a notebook for vocabulary anyway if you are trying to learn the language.) Whether you try to make notes or not, during the course of particularly interesting conversations, you should try to review the major points and key words in your mind so that you can record brief notes later. At the end of each day--and it is important to be regular--you can use these brief notes or key words to record the information in your regular notebooks.

2) The classroom is, of course, one of the best opportunities for learning about the society. As one of the most difficult problems in the classroom is getting each student to talk at length and thus practice his English, it will be most helpful to the student and also interesting to you if you ask questions about topics of particular interest. Certain subjects, especially politics and perhaps religious and other social issues, may be taboo in the classroom, and you definitely should not push into sensitive areas. However, especially if your students are adults, it is most appropriate to ask about many aspects of the society, including myths, history, and economics. Try collecting songs, tales, and sayings. You may want to assign written compositions, or oral reports, on particular topics which interest you. You may want to ask for short autobiographical essays, which give you a sense of the historical experience and personal motivations and world-views of your students. But remember that your first responsibility is to teach, not to exploit captive informants!

3) If you are especially interested in a particular area, for example economics or education, it may be possible to arrange interviews with knowledgeable people. These may be professors or administrators in your school, or they may be government officials, to whom you could be introduced by a friend. Let your interests be known, unless they are likely to lead you into sensitive areas, and try to find out who can help you. Try to seek out local

intellectuals. During your stay, you will surely meet many interesting people; you should try to arrange to visit them again. Explain your interests, perhaps show them a list of questions, and ask permission to make a few notes during your conversation.

4) You should try to establish several appropriate persons as your key informants. Depending on your interests, these may be the mothers in your neighborhood, a few of your students, the administrators in the university, the officials in the government office for economic development, members of student political groups, members of a particular religious group, local artists, and so on. It is better to be able to get to know and to question several people in depth than to converse with many persons briefly, for these purposes. A regular schedule of interviews might be set up. If you know that you will have a chance to talk with someone several times or more, you should try to plan your questions so that you will not offend or somehow alienate the person from the start by asking personal or very difficult questions. Remember that you are first a friend who should not use others for your own ends. Over time, as friendships develop, you will be able to ask questions and learn things which would not be possible initially.

5) There may be less organized and direct means for systematically questioning a particular social group; though you will not be able to make a sociological survey, you may have regular contact with members of some group in which you are interested. For example, in Indonesia, each day you may ride in three or four different *betjaks*; you might use this opportunity to ask each driver several questions about where he was born, when he came to the city, how much he makes in a day, what kind of food he can buy for his family, etc. These questions do not require a great deal of language ability (though understanding the answers might) and could lead to a clearer understanding of many aspects of the local society (in this case, patterns of urbanization and under-employment).

6) It may be a particular advantage to find a friend who would serve as a translator on special occasions. He could accompany you to a special interview or such. Or he could help you translate particular articles from local newspapers. If you arrange for a tutor in the national language, he might help you with this translation.

## Recording Data and Observations

The study guide can serve as a guide for recording data in several ways. You should keep a daily journal, which directly or indirectly attempts to answer and refer to the questions in the study guide. If you have special projects or areas of interest, you should keep separate notebooks for each. Notes from conversations, general observations, or other data should be recorded as soon as possible, preferably each evening. This may require a good deal of time. If it is possible that someone in your house or elsewhere might look through your notebooks and thus cause embarrassment or suspicion, it may be wise to substitute code names for people in your family or for political figures.

Periodically, perhaps every 1-3 months, you should write up a brief report on general observations and tentative conclusions about major issues. It is revealing to look back on these initial observations.

## How Reliable is Your Information?

*One of the major dangers which any traveler faces in visiting another nation is the tendency to generalize on an inadequate number of specific cases.*

—Experiment in International Living
**Observation Guide**

Beware the trap of automatically assuming that because you are given a particular answer to a question, that that *is* the correct answer, or that the particular informant even *thinks* it is the correct answer. Often people, trying to be helpful, would rather give any answer than to tell you that they really don't know. Especially unreliable is any hypothesis or analysis that you yourself have proposed, and to which you have simply received an affirmative reply. Beware of people telling you what they think you want to hear. Ask around, check it out with others who may have a similar perspective, and see if you get the same answer.

**Approach statistics with caution.** What do they really mean? Does the organization that supplied the statistics have a particular bias that might affect these statistics? Do they indirectly measure the success of the organization? Are aid grants dependent on statistics that show progress in this particular area? What important facts about how and why the statistics were collected, might have been withheld from you? Remember that certain kinds of statistics are inherently unreliable. In countries where medical facilities and treatment are spotty, a statistically high incidence of a disease for a particular locality may actually reflect relatively good medical care instead. In areas with a low reported incidence of the same disease, most cases may simply be going untreated.

## General Suggestions

The organization of the study guide might provide a useful basis for a loose filing system for newspaper articles or other printed data which you have collected. The book itself should in no way limit your mode of observation or recording, or keep you from developing your own terminology, categories, and approaches.

This handbook, as it is designed, asks often detailed questions about many major issues. It is quite clear that you will not be able to cover more than a few aspects of these issues in any depth. However, you should review the questions in the handbook periodically in order to recall questions to which answers may be available, and also to help you place what you have learned in a larger framework.

Many of the questions in the handbook deal with national problems, which perhaps can best explored through reading. But your particular opportunity to live in a foreign society best lends itself to a study of microcosms. Through such study of particular situations and problems, you should be able to bring the larger questions into sharper focus.

Finally, you should be very sensitive to political and social issues which are not appropriate for open discussion, especially with a foreigner. You may have to accept the fact that certain information is simply not accessible to you unless you draw suspicion upon yourself, alienate or anger others, and perhaps destroy your effectiveness as a volunteer teacher.

# Economics

Much too often
we forget to listen
to the peasant--the beneficiary,
so to speak, of rural development.

—CERES

# Economics

## Introduction

What is an appropriate cross-cultural approach to economics? Certainly economics involves more than simply material goods. The economic differences between individuals from different societies are more than differences in absolute *standard of living*. Here are two quite different approaches to the *economic problem:*

*...Communities can all be examined within a framework of certain basic facts. Some of the goods and services which people make use of within the community come from outside its boundaries, and money must be paid out of the community for these goods and services. Conversely, some of the goods and services produced within the community eventually go to people outside its borders, and for this, money is paid to people in the community. In addition, people within the community produce goods and services which are consumed within the community. Within the community, there is division of labor both to provide goods and services locally and to produce the things which 'sustain' the community by bringing in the funds which the community needs. So two basic questions underlying a community economic survey would be: What do we produce for ourselves? What do we give to and receive from the rest of the world?*

—Roland L. Warren
**Studying Your Community**

The above writer sees economics primarily as it involves exchange and consumption of goods and services (what goods are being exchanged outside of the community or national unit, and at what rate?). International trade is then seen as $x$ barrels of oil for $y$ bushels of wheat and $z$ pieces of machinery. This gives some insight into actual trade relationships, and the relative money value of workers' time for different nations.

The following passage contains a fundamentally different economic emphasis:

*...the modern economist...is used to measuring the* standard of living *by the amount of annual consumption, assuming all the time that a man who consumes more is* better off *than a man who consumes less. A Buddhist economist would consider this approach excessively irrational: since consumption is merely a means to human well-being, the aim should be to obtain the maximum of well-being with the minimum of consumption.*

—E. F. Schumacher
**Small is Beautiful**

Every society has its own unique economic philosophy. It is important to be sensitive to clues to this philosophy, and to interpret the answers to the following questions with this in mind.

## A. Micro-Economic Circumstances

The following questions concern conditions and activities related to the production and consumption of goods and services at the individual, family, and local level.

1. What are the primary **job activities** of those persons in your immediate community? For each job, note the following:

a. How does the job relate to the larger market structure?

b. What is the individual's income?

c. How many people does he/she support? What relationship do they have with him/her? Why does he/she support them?

d. What is his/her probable background (region of birth, education, ethnic group)? Why did he/she end up with this job?

e. Is the job permanent or temporary? What factors determine whether he/she will continue to hold this job?

f. How does the job rate in terms of social prestige? Does the individual aspire to a better status? What are the factors determining his social mobility?

g. What special skills, resources, or contacts does the job require? How did the individual acquire them?

h. Does the job involve production for home use, monetary return, and/or remuneration in kind?

i. Does the individual hold more than one job? If so, why (money is not always the reason)? How many hours a week does he/she work at each?

2. What is a typical **family budget** for the circumstances with which you are most familiar?

a. What percentage of income goes for food? Rent? Clothing? Transportation? Education? Personal hygiene and health services? Savings? Insurance? Other goods and services?

b. Who contributes to family income? How would the family use extra income if they had it? What does a family do when there is not enough income (e.g. when actual income falls short of expected income)?

3. What are the primary **agricultural activities** in the area?

a. What crops are raised?

b. What animals are raised? For food, use as work

animals, or other reasons?

c. How much time is actually spent planting, harvesting and doing similar direct work in the fields? Is there an *off-season*? Are farmers idle during long periods of time? What do they do at such times?

d. How is work divided among different members of the family, extended family, and community?

e. Are agricultural products primarily used by the immediate family, or marketed?

f. What factors determine selection and output of crops (climate, soil, market conditions, price, transport, demands for labor, demands for equipment, fertilizers, irrigation)?

g. How much land does the individual or family use? Does he own it? What are the conditions of ownership? How did he acquire it and how will he pass it on?

4. What **factories** of any kind or size are in the area? (These may include small home shops and the like.)

a. What do they produce and where do they sell the products?

b. Where do they acquire the materials needed?

c. Who owns the factory? When was it built?

d. What capital equipment does it use? Is the equipment obsolete? If so, why?

e. Is the operation expanding? Why or why not?

f. How many people are employed? How were they recruited? What are their ages, wages, special skills, and working conditions?

g. Are there any types of *union* organizations? If not, why?

5. What are the primary **service activities** in the area (health, education, transportation, finance, civil service, communications, etc.)?

a. What factors affect the size and efficiencies of these activities?

b. How many of these needs are supplied by the immediate or extended family to individuals in a community?

c. Are the services funded by the government or by private groups?

d. What programs seem to be needed? Do the local people agree?

6. To what extent is the local economy or its various sectors **monetized**? How much marketing activity is based on barter? How important are local markets as compared with retail stores? What kind of retail stores exist? Who owns them?

7.a. How are the words **employment** and **unemployment** used? What attitudes toward life and work are embodied in the local concept of employment?

b. What is the real level of unemployment? Underemployment (as manifested by economically and culturally unnecessary work or very low level of activity during working hours)?

c. Are some college graduates unemployed? Why?

8. Is all available labor used productively? How could it be used more productively, from the point of view of the general economy? What effects would this be likely to have on the individuals involved?

---

**Selling its coffee (or copper, or bananas or tea) to the rich world while neglecting its internal and self-directed development, a poor country will remain a marginal land condemned to vulnerability, dependence, and impoverishment.**

**--Samir Amin**

---

9. How do government activities and regulations affect local economic life?

10. To what extent are people interested in savings, accumulation, or entrepreneurship? What motives, attitudes, and aspirations may have some impact on their economic life? Are these changing? Why? If they aren't, why not? If the people themselves want to actively change the above, what factors prevent them from doing so?

11. What is the proportion of children and the aged as economic dependents?

12. In what ways do family ties serve as a form of **social security**?

a. Does this cut down on the accumulation of capital with which needed investment might take place?

b. Does this eliminate the need for, and cost of a bureaucracy to administrate some kind of social security program?

c. What are the strengths and weaknesses of this form of social security?

d. What are the most important threats to the continuation of the family as a social and economic unit?

## B. General Micro-Level Questions

1. Consider the meaning and function of *work:*

*The Buddhist point of view takes the function of work to be at least threefold: to give a man a chance to utilize and develop his faculties; to enable him to overcome his egocenteredness by joining with other people in a common task; and to bring forth the goods and services needed for a becoming existence. Again, the consequences that flow from this view are endless. To organize work in such a manner that it becomes meaningless, boring, stultifying, or nerve-racking for the worker would be little short of criminal; it would indicate a greater concern with goods than with people, an evil lack of compassion and a soul-destroying degree of attachment to the most primitive side of this worldly existence. Equally, to strive for leisure as an alternative to work would be considered a complete misunderstanding of one of the basic truths of human existence, namely that work and leisure are complementary parts of the same living process and cannot be separated without destroying the joy of work and the bliss of leisure.*

—E. F. Schumacher
**Small is Beautiful**

How does the function of work in the society under examination compare to the above? To that in your own society? Which is it most similar to?

2. What kind of person is regarded to be a *good worker*? *Bad worker*?

3. How does the community react towards those who don't work, can't work, or won't work?

4. Towards what ends are the people working? Are they trying to 'get ahead,' or are they 'just living'? Is there the phenomenon of *rising expectations*?

5. How do religious and other **beliefs** affect farming practices?

6. Are many hours of labor being exchanged for foreign luxury items (e.g. hand-made batik cloth for Mercedes automobiles)?

7. Arrange to accompany a peddler on his daily rounds. Describe his activities, the people he deals with, how he interacts with them, and where he lives. A similar approach might be used with others, such as a bus driver or food stall owner.

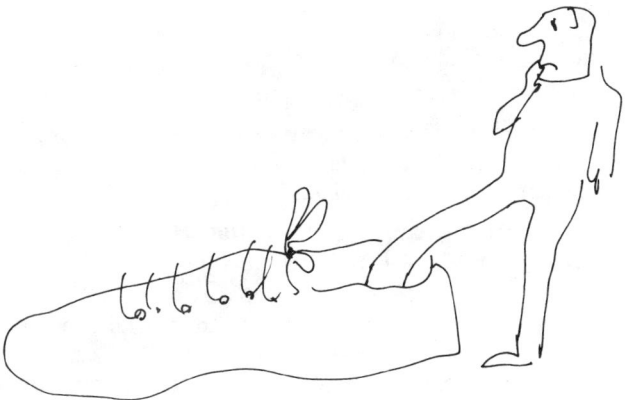

*Imposed patterns of consumption*

## C. Macro-Economic Circumstances

These questions are concerned with the following topics: conditions and activities of the regional and national economy; problems and potentials for economic development; and issues of political economy.

1. What percentage of the **labor force** is involved in agriculture? Industry? Services? Civil service? Armed forces?

a. What organizations and unions (government and non-government) exist for farmers and workers?

b. What are the general living standards for workers? What are average wages (in purchasing power)?

c. What impact does industrial (or agricultural) wage labor have on the social system of the village or small town? How do opportunities in the wage economy influence migration to the cities?

d. What are government, corporate, and union policies on wages? Are there any other worker benefits?

e. How much control, if any, do workers have over the factory or plantation?

f. What are normal working hours?

2. What is the annual **per capita income** for the country? How accurately does this statistic (in dollars) reflect comparative living standards?

3. What is the current **gross national product** for the country? How fast has it been growing?

a. In what ways do economic statistics such as GNP give a distorted view of the economic condition of the country (e.g. what things do not get counted for the GNP, and how might the relative prices of services affect comparative GNP's)?

b. How is GNP distributed among the people? Do all the people share equally in GNP growth, or does it represent an increase in income among the wealthy few only?

c.  If measures such as GNP and *level of employment* are insufficient to gauge the comparative economic health and self-sufficiency of developing areas, what indicators might be more useful or accurate?

---

**The national economy of the period of independence is not set on a new footing. It is still concerned with the groundnut harvest, with the cocoa crop and the olive yield. In the same way there is no change in the marketing of basic products, and not a single industry is set up in the country. We go on sending out raw materials; we go on being Europe's small farmers, who specialize in unfinished products.**

**—Frantz Fanon**

---

4.  What are the primary **agricultural** products of the country? Where are they produced?

a.  Are sufficient foodstuffs produced or must they be imported? Does this vary regionally? If there is an insufficiency, what are the causes (e.g. bad weather, insufficient land, overpopulation, government mismanagement)?

b.  Is the major part of agricultural production distributed through marketing systems or is it consumed by its producers as subsistence?

c.  What agricultural products are exported? Are they processed in any way first? Does the production of agricultural goods for export help to create local food shortages, by pre-empting important crop land? Does it lower the nutritional level of the crops a farmer also raises to feed his family?

d.  How do weather conditions affect the major food staples and the major export commodities? Changes in the world market prices?

e. For certain agricultural products such as copra and rubber, the age of the producing trees is of importance in indicating future production potential. Where do these statistics lead?

f. What are the primary structures for agricultural production (e.g. privately-owned plots, cooperatives, plantations, government-operated collectives)? What are the advantages and disadvantages of each, in terms of output, costs, well-being of workers, potential for growth, self-sufficiency, etc.? Who owns the plantations, if any? How have each of the structures developed over time? Was plantation land once owned by the peasants?

g. What is the present distribution of land? What is the average size of private landholdings? Is this changing over time? Is the land worked by the owners? Share-croppers? Wage laborers? How are class structures reflected in landholdings? Is land reform a political issue? If so, how effective is it in changing the people's lives for the better? Does land reform really exist?

h. What scientific or technological innovations (e.g. IR8 rice) have already, or could potentially, improve the lives of the people in the rural areas? Could new crops produce an economic advantage? Are there government or other projects to promote improved agricultural techniques? How successful have they been? What problems have they encountered? How receptive are the farmers to these innovations?

i. What is the government policy regarding agriculture? Are small farms encouraged?

5. What and where are the major **natural resources** of the country?

a. To what extent are they presently exploited? By whom?

b. Are they used locally, or exported?

c. Are there refineries within the country? Are new ones

being built? What percentage of production is refined within the country? Is this increasing? If not, why not? What percentage of production is for domestic use? Is any of this refined *outside* the country, and shipped back to it for use?

d. Are natural resources under public, private domestic, or foreign ownership?

e. Are there any *internal colonies* in the country related to natural resources?

f. Who benefits most from the income generated by natural resources exploitation?

6. Is there a national **energy policy**? What energy sources does the government plan to develop?

a. What is the level of production of crude oil? What percentage is refined within the country? What percentage is used domestically? Is some oil shipped to foreign refineries and then re-imported at higher prices? How much exploration is going on? By whom? Where is exported oil shipped? Why?

b. What are the effects of high oil prices on: national foreign exchange holdings; the use of petrochemical fertilizers and other elements of agricultural production; the use of autos, motorcycles, trucks, buses, and trains; the supply and cost of kerosene for home stoves?

c. What are the other important sources of energy? Nuclear? Hydroelectric? Natural gas? Wood? Coal? Are they domestically available or imported?

7. What are the most important **industries** in the country?

a. What heavy industries have been established? Who owns and operates them? How viable is their economic position? What percentage of their output is used domestically, and how much is exported?

b. Are there processing plants for primary products such as rubber, sugar, and minerals? What factors influence the development of such plants?

c. Are there assembly plants in the country? Where? To what extent do they depend on imported parts? Who owns them? If they are foreign-owned, why did the foreign companies choose to locate the plants where they did?

d. What handicrafts industries exist? Are they operated as family industries or as larger enterprises? Are their products exported? Do the artisans get a fair return for their work?

---

**As a measure of internal growth, the annual change in GNP is adequate; for comparing nations it is at best extremely crude; but as a measure of authentic development, it is virtually worthless.**

**--Mauritz Sundt Mortersen**

---

e. How advanced is the technology of the various industries? Do they employ foreign technicians? Where were the national technicians trained? What are the prospects for nationals to take greater responsibility within these industries?

f. Is the domestic manufacture of goods appealing to the consumer public? If not, why not?

g. To what extent does the country depend on importing capital goods, machinery, trucks, and buses? What does it import? From whom? How modern is this equipment? Are replacement parts available? At what cost? If equipment is old and/or imported from a number of different countries, what parts problems does this create? What standardization of measurements problems? How are these problems dealt with?

h. Which of the above can be manufactured domestically?

i. To what extent could technologically less sophisticated

and less expensive equipment and machinery be used, especially for small, local industries in towns and villages?

j. To what extent are industries capital-intensive (i.e requiring large investments in expensive equipment and utilizing relatively little labor) rather than labor-intensive? Are capital-intensive industries most advantageous, considering the labor force available? What are the limitations and disadvantages of labor-intensive industries and projects?

*This could be done equally well by hand*

k. What is the general growth rate of the industrial-manufacturing sector of the economy? Which industries are growing fastest? Why?

l. Which industries receive government support (e.g. tax benefits, subsidies, controls over foreign competition)? Why?

m. Who owns the various industrial enterprises? Under what legal structures?

8. What is the role of **foreign investment** in the country?

a. Which foreign corporations have investments in the country? How much? In what industries? How long have these investments existed?

b. How capital-intensive are these operations? Where is the necessary capital equipment produced?

c. How does the government regulate foreign investment? What is their general policy and attitude toward it?

d. To what extent do foreign companies use 1) trained personnel, and 2) other labor from the country? Does the government have quotas or schedules for employment of nationals? What is the ratio of investment to number of jobs created?

e. How important and influential are the foreign corporations within the whole economy?

f. What special revenues (e.g. taxes and duties) are earned from foreign companies?

g. What are the terms of the contracts under which the foreign corporations operate in the country?

h. What would happen if the foreign investments were nationalized? What would be the economic consequences in terms of trained personnel, operating capital, and marketing connections? What would be the political consequences?

i. Are there many *joint ownership* operations? Does the government require this in some cases? Who really controls these joint ownership operations?

j. In general, do you think that the presence of foreign corporations is an advantage to the country as a whole? Or does this advantage accrue only to the government and business strata of the society? To what extent do the foreign corporations, independently or through their own national governments, exert political influence in the country?

9. What are the major **exports** of the country? Are they primary, processed, or manufactured products?

a. What are the conditions of the world markets for these goods? Have prices for each product been stable, rising, or falling over the past 10-30 years?

b. For agricultural products particularly, have world markets been undergoing qualitative changes (e.g. jute being replaced by other products)?

c. How do weather conditions affect these agricultural commodities?

d. For certain agricultural products such as copra and rubber, the age of the producing trees is an important indicator of future production potential. What do these statistics imply for the future?

e. Are there any external constraints on exports (e.g. import quotas or tariffs in the United States and Europe)? What impact do they have?

f. Are there any domestic constraints on exports (e.g. duties or license requirements)? What impact do they have?

g. Who controls most export activities?

10. What are the major **imports** of the country?

a. How does the government regulate imports (e.g. duties, tariffs, quotas, licenses)?

b. Is there considerable smuggling?

c. Does the present level of imports meet the needs for capital equipment which cannot be produced within the country?

d. What is the effect of government policies on imports? Do they encourage import substitution industries? Do they hinder luxury consumption by elites? Do the tariffs protect 'infant' industries? Could this be done more effectively by subsidies or tax incentives rather than tariffs?

11. What are the sources of **foreign exchange** for the

country? Exports? Loans? Foreign grants? Taxes on foreign companies? Earnings of nationals living abroad?

a. In what foreign currencies does the government have holdings?

b. Why is foreign exchange so important?

c. Is the currency tied to any major international currency? Why?

12. Are there many **cooperatives** operating in the economy? What kind (e.g. consumer, health, insurance, purchasing, marketing, community work)? What is their structure? Who runs them? If coops fail, why?

13. What are the primary **marketing** structures at all levels?

a. For imports and exports, what external sources control the world market, especially for primary products such as sugar, oil, timber, and minerals? How do these affect volume, prices, and net revenue? What or who controls these external market structures?

b. In the modern, largely urban sectors of the economy, what market structures exist for buying, transporting, wholesaling, retailing, and pricing goods? What parts of the structure are controlled by the government? Are there any price controls, rationed goods, or illegal luxury items? What parts of the structure are controlled by large, private corporations or enterprises? By local minorities (e.g. the Chinese in Indonesia and the Philippines)?

c. How do prices vary between the modern, urban sectors and the village sectors? How is marketing handled in the village or in the non-modern sectors of the urban economy? What goods are available in these markets? How are they acquired and delivered?

14. How are products **recycled** and re-used? Are they repaired? Are they used for different purposes than the original ones? What kinds of things are not re-used?

What kinds of things that are thrown away in your own country, are *not* thrown away here? Why? What effects does this have on the environment and on the economy?

15.  What is the condition of the national **infrastructure** and how quickly is it being improved? Infrastructure-- physical capital which must service all industrial development--includes systems for transportation, communication, power production, electrification, water supply, and irrigation development. Who does the infrastructure serve?

a.  If a former colony is being studied, has infrastructure maintenance and development increased, decreased, or shifted in emphasis with independence? (A former colony with important ore deposits might have excellent infrastructure facilities for all aspects of mining. However, these facilities may not meet the needs of the people. Roads in such a case might run from the mines to the coast, facilitating ore export, but be lacking between populated regions. In the latter case they are important for transport and communications; stability and security by preventing famine due to local crop failures; and access to medical care.)

b.  The development and control of infrastructure is usually the responsibility of the government. To what extent is this true in this country? How efficiently is the infrastructure managed?

c.  Are labor-intensive projects used to build roads, dams, etc.? If not, why not? If so, who manages them? How are they financed (labor and materials)? What is the quality and the durability of the materials used? How do those who work on the projects feel about them?

d.  Is the irrigation system, if any, adequate and properly maintained? Could improvement in irrigation substantially improve agricultural output in some regions? How does the village or local community usually manage irrigation? Can government-initiated programs be of use? Consider both the harmful and beneficial aspects of flooding.

e. What are the primary power sources for the country-- hydroelectric, coal, oil? Where are the fuels obtained? How modern are the power plants? What is the frequency of the use of small generators?

f. Is lack of infrastructure a major impediment toward growth in agriculture, marketing, industry, and resource exploitation?

g. Do foreign companies participate in infrastructure development? What kind of infrastructure? Who does it benefit? What are the incentives?

h. What changes would be brought about in the villages if increased communication links, roads, and electricity were available?

i. Are there any people-initiated infrastructure programs? What and who started these?

---

## Industrialized food production is so costly that it is simply beyond the reach of the poorer countries.
### --Georg Borgstrom

---

16. Does the national government coordinate and provide for economic growth; that is, is there **centralized government planning**?

a. Has the government prepared Development Plans or something comparable? What are the stated priorities, policies, and goals of the present plan? Are they realistic? How well have the goals of past plans been realized? Who prepares the plan? Are there foreign advisors? How 'visible' are they? Through what ministries and bureaucracies is the plan implemented? To what extent and in what ways does the plan depend upon the cooperation or regulation of private enterprise? Has the plan been well publicized and does it have public support and confidence? Does the plan help to mobilize people for economic efforts? To what extent do figures of 'miles of roads built' and the like simply reflect normal replacement rates?

b. If the government has no centralized, long-term planning, what are its stated economic goals and policies? Is there local government planning?

17. What industries and enterprises does the government own and operate? How large is this **public sector** compared to the private sector?

a. Why is the government active in these particular industries and projects?

b. How efficiently is the public sector operated? Is there much corruption?

c. What advantages and/or disadvantages (economic, social, and political) are there to government ownership?

d. Does the military participate in the economy? In what ways?

18. What is the present **government budget**?

a. What are the absolute and percentage allocations for the major expenditures?

b. Compare these expenditures to those of your own government.

c. Does the government subsidized food imports on a massive scale? What effects does this have on the economy? Are there other subsidized imports?

19. What are the primary sources of **government revenues**?

a. What taxes does the government levy (e.g. property, income, sales, and private business taxes)? How efficiently are they collected? What are the problems of tax administration? Are taxes *progressive* and thus fall more heavily on the rich? How can the rich avoid paying taxes? What percentage of revenues come from taxes?

b. How much revenue is earned through export duties and import tariffs?

c. How much do government-owned industries and enterprises contribute to general revenue?

d. How does the government raise money through fees for permits, licenses, services, etc.?

20. What **foreign aid** does the government receive? From whom, in what form, and on what terms? Does the aid consist of grants, loans, food, equipment, or advisors?

a. How much military aid is received?

b. What economic or political 'strings' are attached to the aid? Does the donor nation require that the recipient buy products from it, or use its shipping?

c. If aid were cut off, what would be the effect?

d. Is the aid for specific projects or for the general economic program of the government? If it is for specific projects, what kind, and why?

e. Does the donor nation determine the use of the aid?

f. Does foreign aid in foreign currencies lead to an increase in the importation of machinery or other goods, rather than internal development?

g. What is the effect of the aid on the country's political and social balance?

h. How much of this foreign aid goes into public use?

i. How much of the government's finances come from abroad in the form of loans, grants, or other aid? Does this country have large outstanding debts to foreign governments, international consortiums, or the World Bank? What are the interest rates, repayment schedules, and other terms? What are the implications of these for the future?

j. Does food aid lead to dependency, and postpone real change in government policy with respect to the rural areas?

21. What are the sources and structures for domestic **savings** and capital accumulation?

a. Do individuals have sufficient income and incentive to save a fraction rather than consume all of their income? Are these savings deposited in banks or invested in some other way? What is the general attitude towards such saving?

b. How do private entrepreneurs and corporations acquire capital for investment? Do they have access to external money markets? Do they constitute a preferred investment for domestic investors?

---

**Implicit in the conventional concept of aid is that internal problems may be remedied by the transfer of goods, services, or knowledge from external sources; in true development, internal problems call up internal remedies.**

### --Julius Nyerere

---

c. What are the government and private banking structures? Are all purchases 'cash and carry'? Is credit available to consumers? What are the current interest rates for deposits, loans, etc.? What policies control banking practices?

d. How are these structures related to foreign or international banking structures?

22. Is **tourism** an important industry in this country?

a. Who sponsors the tourist industry? Does the government regulate it? Toward what ends?

b. How much income--especially foreign exchange--does tourism provide for the country? Who gets this income? How does the presence of a tourist sector affect other sectors of the economy and the society in general?

What do you think the best policy would be toward tourism?

c. What are the infrastructure expenditures for tourism (e.g. restoration of historical buildings and temples, government sponsored construction of hotels, airport facilities, etc.)?

23. Has the country experienced **inflation** in recent years? At what rate? What caused it? What were the effects--on individuals of various classes, and on the general economy? What policies have been established to combat it, if any?

24. What are the economic forces which cause **urbanization**? Are there regulations that directly encourage or discourage movement to the cities? What are the social, economic, and political effects of urbanization? How could this process be controlled? Should it be?

25. What has been the impact of **population growth** on economic conditions and development? What is the present growth rate? What projections can be made? How extensive and/or successful are the activities of family planning organizations? (See *Family Planning* under *HEALTH* and *SOCIAL STRUCTURE*.)

26. What seems to be the relationship between **economic and political power**? What are the inter-relationships between the most wealthy and the most politically influential elites? To what extent are political policies and economic programs developed primarily in the interests of economic elites?

27. Is the country a member of any **regional economic planning groups**, such as ECAFE or ASEAN? What are the structures, purposes, problems, and accomplishments of these organizations? What bilateral or multi-lateral trade agreements or economic policies affect the nation's economy?

# D. General Macro-Level Questions

1. *A most important problem in the second half of the twentieth century is the geographical distribution of population, the question of 'regionalism.' But regionalism, not in the sense of combining a lot of states into free-trade systems, but in the opposite sense of developing all the regions within each country. This, in fact, is the most important subject on the agenda of all the larger nations today. And a lot of the nationalism of small nations today, and the desire for self-government and so-called independence, is simply a logical and rational response to the need for regional development. In the poor countries in particular there is no hope for the poor unless there is successful regional development, a development effort outside the capital city covering all the rural areas wherever people happen to be.*

—E. F. Schumacher
**Small is Beautiful**

To what extent is the pattern of economic development *nodular*, i.e., concentrated in particular regions or urban centers of the country? Is this inevitable? What are the political, economic, and social effects of uneven development?

2. What observations can you make on the total impact of economic development on the social structure, political system, cultural forms, and traditional values of the country? (The *traditional, indigenous* nature of these elements may be misleading after 200 years of colonialism.) What value judgement do you place on this? How do most nationals appraise and judge the process of economic development?

3. How applicable does a Western economic model and its terminology seem to be to the objective realities and the cultural forms of the country? How could a Marxist model be applied? How would its goals differ from those

implicit in a Western model? How could a decentralist economic model, such as that of Gandhi, be applied? What other models could be used? Why could they be more desirable?

4. How would the process and problems of economic development look different to an anthropologist looking from the village up, as opposed to an economist looking from the capital down? To what extent is development a social-psychological-cultural question rather than a purely economic problem? Conversely, can new ideas alone really lead to development?

5. How do you personally respond to the economic problems of this nation? Do you consider them to be *differences* and not *problems*? Or, is the situation *their* problem, not yours?

6. *You're either part of the problem or part of the solution.* Do you agree with this statement? Which are you? If you are part of the problem, how can you change that?

7. Do you have a more concrete idea of how development in this country will take place? What is different about your present understanding? Why? What are your priorities for development in the area in which you live?

8. A Quaker group cautions:

*Unfortunately, most humanitarian programs to end United States and world poverty take little or no account of the eco-system. They implicitly assume that it would be good if all American and world poor were brought to something like the average American standard of consumption and that this rate of consumption could continue to increase more or less indefinitely.*

*Yet scientists are telling us that, if everyone in the world consumed at the present rate of most Americans, not only would most of the world's key resources be depleted within a few decades, but mankind might soon become extinct from the resulting imbalances of nature.*

*The goal of a happy, high-consumption world cannot be fulfilled even for the 3.5 billion people now alive, much less the 6 billion expected by the year 2000. ...At the American standard of living, the earth could support only 500 million.*

Discuss the above, in the light of your answer to question seven. What implications does this have for the United States, the other developed nations, and the developing nations, as members of a world community?

*'The investment process,' or 'Them that has, gets'*

# Politics

**Politics and development:
two concepts
that have been kept
separate for too long.**

**--CERES**

# Politics

## I. NATIONAL AND INTERNATIONAL

### A. Description

The following questions are intended to facilitate the gathering of factual information describing national politics and foreign policy.

1. What are the **legally established functions** of the political institutions?

a. What form does the executive part of the government take? What are its powers prescribed by law? What form does the country's constitution take? How did it come into being, and who wrote it? What are the relationships between the executive and the military, the legislative, and the judicial branches? If these categories are not useful, how would you describe the various bodies that constitute the government? Within the executive branch, how is this broad function divided into ministries and departments? How do these departments relate to one another in theory? What is the role of government officials in the formulation of laws? How are they paid?

b. Is there a legislature? What powers is it given under law? Does it have a check on the executive or the military? How is the legislature convened, and by whom? How often does it meet, and who governs its procedures? What is its committee structure, if any? How much are legislators paid?

c. Is there a judiciary? Is it separate from the executive? What are its constitutional powers? Its civil and penal powers? How are its members paid?

d. Is there a political party designated by law? What form does the party apparatus take? How independent from the national governmental structure is the party? Is it issue-oriented or built around a group or personal relations? How is the party supported? How are its officials paid?

2. What are the **actual functions** of the political institutions?

a. Is there in practice a separation between the executive branch, the military, the legislature, and the judiciary? If not, which is the most powerful, and how is that power manifested in appointments, influence, and corruption? Is the executive branch serving one class, one ethnic group, or one region? Within the executive branch, are there conflicts between departments? Which ministry is the most influential? How do they check and limit each others' power?

b. Does the legislature utilize its delegated powers? Is it an effective check on the military and/or the executive? What interests are represented in the legislature? Which are the most powerful? How are conflicts within the body resolved? Is the legislature representative of the country as a whole? How can the legislature or individual legislators effect change in government policy, domestic or foreign?

c. Is the judiciary impartial or does it serve any special interests? How do its pronouncements affect domestic and foreign policy?

d. How does the local government relate to the national government's local bureaucracy? How are conflicts between the two resolved? How much do national issues affect local governments? Are local governments in all cases representative of the immediate constituency? How much influence do local officials have in determining policies, domestic or foreign?

e. How many political parties are there nationally? Why did they form? Does one have a preponderance of power? What are their ideologies and programs? How are they supported? How are campaigns conducted? What types of issues, slogans, and accusations are common? To which groups are appeals directed? Do parties reflect class, ethnic, or regional interests?

f. What types of interest groups are there? How do interest groups articulate their concerns to the legislature, executive branch, military, and judiciary? What role does corruption play? If there are foreign private interest groups, do their interests affect foreign relations, particularly with their home country? How do interest groups pressure the government or political parties? How is conflict between interest groups resolved?

---

**...it is a commonplace to observe and to say that in the majority of cases, for ninety-five percent of the population of underdeveloped countries, independence brings no immediate change. The enlightened observor takes note of the existence of a kind of masked discontent like the smoking ashes of a burnt-down house after the fire has been put out, which still threaten to burst into flames again.**

**--Frantz Fanon**

---

3. Who are the individuals that exercise the executive, legislative, and judicial powers?

a. From what class, ethnic group, religion, and region do these people come? How typical are their backgrounds compared with leaders the nation has had in the past? Do they represent parties or interest groups? What ties of personal loyalty exist between decisionmakers? Would you characterize the political bonds as *affective* or *rational*? How are personal ambitions manifested and resolved? What happens when conflict arises between two individuals?

4. How does the political structure reproduce itself?

a. How do individuals enter the political system? What rewards are there? What risks?

b. How much mobility is there in the government or party structure? On what factors does mobility depend?

c. How and who initiates institutional change? How long does it usually take? Can it be used to mollify interest groups? Is reform ever substantial?

d. Without institutional change, can individuals augment their power in the government or party structure? How is that accomplished? What roles in the government or party have prestige but little responsibility?

5. What **values and attitudes** are encouraged at the national level?

a. From what sources do they come?

b. Is stability encouraged? Is conformity the price of involvement at the national level? What values do the civil service and political parties foster?

c. Do the values of the leaders clash with those of the people they govern? How are conflicts between institutional and personal values resolved?

d. What methods are used to propagate a political ideology? What is taught in schools about national politics and foreign policy? How is political socialization tied in with the propagation of religious, class, ethnic, or regional values?

e. Who controls the press? The radio? How effective are these two means of communication in socializing people? What effect do language differences have?

f. Is any one group in the country looked to for leadership in politics? Does concern with raising one's status or retaining it play upon political attitudes?

g. Do foreign interests attempt public relations work

within the country? What forms does this take? How is it received by the people, the government, the military, and the political parties?

6. What are the **political myths** of this country?

a. Is there a 'father' of the country? How are historical heroes lionized? What makes them heroes?

b. What kinds of myths about the political process are there? What function do they serve? How many people believe them?

c. Are religious, class, or ethnic myths used by the government, political parties, or military to achieve political ends? What kinds of myths are they? What is their origin?

7. What **demands** are made upon the political institutions?

a. Are the demands mainly economic, social, or political (e.g. demands for lower taxes, integration, or voting rights)?

b. Who is allowed to make a demand? Who in practice makes them?

c. What channels for input are open between: interest groups and the state; local government and national government; and individuals and their party? How valuable are those channels? Are there extra-legal, religious, or personal channels?

d. How frequently are demands made upon the political structure?

e. Are demands made by foreign interests? Through what channels? For what reasons? How successful are they, and why?

f. What are the costs of making a demand? Are individuals endangered? Are groups or parties outlawed?

g. How does the response of the political institution correspond to the demand? Does the means of response indicate anything about the demand and its effects on the political structure?

8. What are the kinds of support given to the political structure?

a. Who pays taxes? What kinds of taxes are there? Can one avoid paying taxes if one wants to? Is this act political or economic in its motivation? How does the method of taxation relate to political sanctions? Are taxes progressive or regressive? What groups are taxed disproportionately?

b. Are there government monopolies? Over what industries? Does this have political significance as it relates to a specific class or group? Does this involve corruption?

c. Does the press support government, party, or military policies? Why? How effective is this support?

d. What interest groups support the government, and for what reasons?

e. What foreign countries supply the greatest amount of aid to the country? In what forms? How popular is that aid? How does the government utilize the support given by a foreign interest? What strings are attached?

f. Is there any active opposition to the government, party, or military? For what reasons? Do these groups withdraw tacit support of the government?

9. What political **sanctions** exist?

a. Are there any statutes outlawing political acts or statements? What are the penalties? What is the history of these laws? Are they still necessary? Who defends them?

b. Within the executive branch, the military, the party structure, and the legislature, is there a written or unwritten code forbidding certain political acts or statements? What are the penalties and consequences for the individual who breaks this code? Is the code effective? Who enforces it?

c. Are there legal or institutional sanctions against corruption? What are the penalties? What is the history of these sanctions? Are they effective?

d. Are people ostracized for their political beliefs? Are they threatened or intimidated personally?

e. What pressures can an interest group bring upon its representatives?

## B. Analysis

The following questions are intended to stimulate critical thinking about information gathered in the preceding section.

1. If one religious, ethnic, class, or regional group is in control of a political institution, why is it allowed to maintain that control? What means, legal and otherwise, does it use to maintain its control? What function does corruption serve in perpetuating the governing group? Religious prejudices? Foreign interests? How does this oligarchical structure affect political life in the country?

2. What bias does the recruitment of individuals into the political structure possess? Is it economic, social, religious, ethnic, or regional? Why does this bias exist? What purpose does it serve/ How does it affect the country and the stated goals of the government?

3. Whom does **stability** serve? For what reasons?

4. How do various interest groups relate to each other (e.g. foreign oil interests and nationalistic students; Buddhists and bureaucrats)? Do coalitions spring up among any interest groups? Are these in support of specific demands? Against government or party policy? Do coalitions last long? What compromises are made? What personalities are involved?

5. Are parties centered around a program, ideology, or a particular charismatic personality? If there is a religion associated with any party, why? How do different parties or factions treat the issue of *nationalism vs. the need for foreign investment for development*? How do different parties or factions feel about the traditional culture of the

country and the threat posed by modernization and 'Western youth values'? Do all factions or political parties make appeals to all ethnic-religious-class groups within the country? If not, why not? Can you find contradictions in a party's platform?

6. Has any group within the country been **oppressed**? Why? What are the origins of this? What effects has this had on the country?

7. How well do participants in the political structure cater to or mirror popular beliefs and attitudes about religion, social customs of a particular class, and ethnic traditions? How and why do they do this?

8. How are demands reflected in policy?

a. What seems to be the best method of putting forth a demand? Who or which group seems to possess the most domestic influence? Does this stem from their economic, religious, or social status? Try to illuminate the channel of influence?

---

**As powerful classes organize a nation, so powerful nations organize a crude society of nations. In each case the peace is a tentative one because it is unjust.**

**--Reinhold Niebuhr**

---

b. How large an influence do foreign interests have over national policy? How does this affect the government's credibility with students, intellectuals, the military, the bureaucracy, and the peasantry?

c. Do national groups draw upon international or foreign groups for support in making demands upon the national government? How does this support manifest itself? What do local groups give up in return?

9. How are **supports** maintained?

a. How compulsory are taxes? What groups do they favor, and why? What groups do they exploit, and why?

b. How does the government justify the collection of taxes? Defense? Development? How much is their reasoning challenged?

c. How does the government justify nationalizing industries? Permitting foreign investment? Receiving foreign aid? Who challenges these things and for what reasons?

d. How much does the government and/or party depend on interest groups for support? What form does that support take? Is the support absolute or issue-oriented?

e. Why are supports necessary? What is the relationship between the demands of a group and the supports it gives to the government or party?

10. What is the policy of the country toward regional ties, the United Nations, foreign investment, the Indochina War, China, Russia, Japan, Europe, and the U.S.? What are the differences between verbal and actual foreign policy? How is foreign policy determined? Put into effect? How successful, in its own terms, has it been?

11. Analyze the reactions of the following to one or a number of recent government policy decisions: a petty bureaucrat, an influential minority leader, a party official, a shopkeeper, and a peasant.

## C. Future Possibilities

The following questions are focused on national political trends.

1. How will the political structure develop or change?

a. What will be the future of the various political parties? Why?

b. How will the power of the executive change in the

next year? Why? What are the future fortunes of government bureaucrats?

c. What is the future of foreign investments in the country? Foreign influence? Why?

d. What interest groups will decline in importance? How will the student movement change? What growing religious movements have political significance for the future? How will anticipated changes in the economy in the next year affect political ambitions? What are the prospects for the radical or communist left? Why?

e. What kinds of governmental or military reforms are likely? Why? What will the consequences be?

f. How will predicted trends in the foreign policy of the U.S., China, Japan, Russia, and the European nations affect the domestic and foreign policy of the country? Why?

g. What new laws relating to politics are likely? What will be the consequences of the use of sanctions for partisan reasons?

h. What is the future of corruption in the bureaucracy? Will those groups opposing continued corruption change the nature of their demands in the next year or so?

i. What personalities might be gone from the political scene due to death, assassination, or election defeat? What will the consequences be? Why? What new personalities are rising?

j. What will the issues be in the next campaign? Why?

k. What kinds of conflicts might arise within the executive branch? The legislature? The judiciary? The military? Between these groups?

2. How will the political culture change?

a. What will be the effect of increased contact with Western ideas on the political attitudes of the country? How will these changed attitudes alter the demands made upon the structure and the methods used to make demands? Why?

b. Looking at the domestic or international situation, what new values (e.g. security, national prestige, peace) might arise in the near future? How would these affect the political parties, foreign relations, and the governmental structure?

c. How will increased awareness of ethnic distinctions affect parties, types of demands made, foreign relations, and the governmental structure?

d. Will the political atmosphere become more or less constrained? Why? What will be the consequences?

e. Can a *class awareness* develop? Why? What would be the consequences? Why?

f. What new policies in the educational and economic realms might have political repercussions?

3. How will the political process change?

a. Will methods of making demands become more or less violent? Why? How will this change the responses of the government and the political parties to demands?

b. What types of changes do you foresee in the types of campaigns waged? Types of issues raised?

c. Will intellectuals become more or less involved in the political process? If less, will this lead to alienation? What will the consequences be? Why? If they become more involved, will this lead to conflict? Why? What will the consequences be?

d. What new financial supports will the government seek and find? Will taxes be raised or lowered?

e. Will foreign aid continue in its present form? What will be the repercussions?

f. Will there be a change in the use of financial supports?

g. How will the government's relationship to the economy change? Will there be more nationalization of industries, subsidies, or attempts to attract foreign investment? Discuss the consequences of each of these.

h. From what interest groups will the government need support in the next few years? How will it cultivate that support? What new interest groups (e.g. a middle class) may be forming? What will be the likely consequences?

i. From what foreign countries will the government seek support? In what form? How will it cultivate that support?

4. Outline the reactions of other nations in the same region, the U.S., Japan, Russia, China, and the European nations to the foreign policy trends as you see them in the country under study. What are the reasons for the different reactions? How will the reactions of the foreign nations in turn affect the foreign policy of the country under study?

---

**The fundamental duel which seemed to be that between colonialism and anticolonialism, and indeed between capitalism and socialism, is already losing some of its importance. What counts today, the question which is looming on the horizon, is the need for a redistribution of wealth. Humanity must reply to this question, or be shaken to pieces by it.**

**--Frantz Fanon**

---

## II. PROVINCIAL AND LOCAL

### A. Description

The following questions are intended to facilitate the gathering of factual information describing provincial or local politics.

1. What is the **form** of the local government? What are its functions? Do these functions overlap with those of the national government? How are the officials paid? What is the relation between the various branches of the local government? In theory? In practice?

2. Are there **political parties** particular to this area of the country? Are there local structures for national parties? What form do they take? How are they supported? How independent from the national party headquarters, or national party politics are they? How do they campaign? What kinds of issues are raised? How do they differ from national politics?

3. Are local politics **dominated** by any one group or family? What is the effect of corruption on local politics? Are local politics dominated by a different group than national politics? If so, what conflicts arise? How are they resolved? How does the local government relate to the national government's local bureaucracy? How much do national issues affect local government's efforts to achieve its goals in the immediate area? Is your local government representative of the local constituency?

4. What kinds of **interest groups** are particular to your locality? What are their programs? How are they supported? How do they conduct their business of influencing the political decision-makers? How is conflict between interest groups resolved?

5. Who are the **individuals** that exercise power through the local political structure? From what class, ethnic

group, or religion do these people come? How typical are their backgrounds compared with national leaders, and with leaders the locality has had in the past? Do they represent parties or interest groups?

6. What ties of **personal loyalty** exist between decision-makers? Would you characterize these political bonds as *affective* or *rational*? How are personal ambitions manifested, and realized? What happens when conflict arises between two individuals?

7. How do individuals enter the political system? What rewards are there in local political life? What risks? What is the channel for recruitment from the local government to the national government?

8. How much **mobility** is there in the government or party structure? On what factors does mobility depend?

9. How and who initiates **institutional change**? How long does it usually take? Can it be used to mollify interest groups? Is reform ever substantial?

10. Without institutional change, can individuals augment their power in the local government or party structure? How is that accomplished? Are there any roles in the local government or party structure that are prestigious but do not involve responsibilities?

11. What local **values** contrast with those operating at the national level? From what sources do they come?

12. Is **stability** encouraged? Is conformity the price of involvement at the local level? What values does the local government foster?

13. Do the values of the leaders clash with those of the people they govern? How are conflicts between institutional and personal values resolved (e.g. is doing favors for friends and family members institutionally unacceptable)?

14. What methods are used to propagate a political

ideology? What is taught in schools about the local political structure?

15. Is there local radio? Local TV? Local newspapers? Who controls the **local media**? Does the viewpoint expressed differ from that of the national media? Does the press support or challenge the local officialdom? What kind of people follow the local media carefully? How effective does the media seem to be in socializing people?

16. Is there a **local political mythology**? What heroes are particular to your locality? What makes them heroes? What kinds of myths about the political process are there? What function do they serve? How many people believe them? Are religious myths used by the local party or government to achieve political ends? What kinds of myths are they and what are their origins?

17. How is **political socialization** tied in with the propagation of religious, ethnic, or regional values?

18. What **demands** are made upon local governments?

a. Who makes them? What are they? How often do they occur; how often are they successful? How are they made?

b. What are the costs of making a demand? Are individuals muzzled, harrassed, or jailed?

c. What forms do demands take? Which are the most effective, and for what reasons? Are all avenues of input open to all groups or individuals?

19. What forms of **financial support** are given to the local political structure?

a. Is the local government supported by taxation? Are taxes direct, or does money flow down from the national government (or both)? Can one avoid paying taxes? Is this a political or economic act of defiance? How does the tax structure relate to the use of political sanctions? Are taxes progressive or regressive? What groups are taxed disproportionately? How are taxes collected?

b.  What other sorts of financial support does the government have at the local level? Are there local monopolies which the government runs at a profit? Is corruption viewed as a financial support for the local bureaucracy or is it more individually practiced?

20.  What forms of **political support** are given to the local government?

a.  Does the local press support the government, party or local enforcement agency? Why? How effective is this support? What forms does it take? What strings are attached to this support?

b.  What interest groups support the local government? Why? What forms does this support take? What strings are tied to their support?

---

> **I sit on a man's back choking him and making him carry me and yet assure myself and others that I am sorry for him and wish to lighten his load by all possible means-- except by getting off his back.**
>
> **--Leo Tolstoy**

---

c.  Is there any active opposition to the local government's policies? Why? Who are these people? How do they oppose the government? How effective are they?

d.  How does the local government or individuals within it foster support for its policies? What is taught in the schools about the political process and the political structure?

21.  What **political sanctions** exist?

a.  Are there political sanctions at the local level which do not exist nationally? Why? What are they? Are some national sanctions moderated or enforced more rigorously at the local level?

b. Are individuals ostracized for their political beliefs? What form does this take? What pressures do interest groups bring to bear upon their members to support them?

c. Are there legal or societal sanctions against corruption? What are the local penalties? Are they effective?

## B. Analysis

The following questions are intended to stimulate critical thinking about information gathered in the preceding section:

1. On the local level, what biases does the **recruitment** of individuals into the political structure possess? Whose or what purposes does it serve? How does it affect the political culture of the locality?

2. Whom does **stability** in the locality serve? Why? Whom does a more fluid political situation serve? Why? How do both groups attempt to create the kind of political environment they wish to have?

3. How do the various local interest groups (e.g. businessmen, large landowners, government bureaucrats, and poor peasants) relate to each other? Do **coalitions** spring up among groups? Are these coalitions tied to one issue or are they long-term? What compromises are made? What personalities are involved?

4. Are **local parties** centered around personalities, ideologies, or programs? Why? How do different parties or factions treat the issue of local needs versus national needs? What is their view of the future of the area? Do all parties make appeals to all ethnic, religious, and social groups? Why?

5. Could you say that one group in the locality is being

discriminated against? Oppressed? How? Why? What are the effects on the political culture of that one sub-group and of the whole locality?

6. How well do participants in the local political structure mirror local beliefs and attitudes about religion, social customs, and ethnic traditions? To what purpose? Contrast their attitudes with those of the national government leaders.

7. How are **demands** reflected in policy?

a. What seems to be the best method of making a demand? Who or which group possesses the most influence? Try to illuminate the channel of influence. What costs must this group bear for its access to the government decision-making process?

b. What justifications does the structure give for turning down demands? What are the repercussions?

8. How are **supports** maintained?

a. How compulsory are taxes? What groups do they favor, and why? What groups do they exploit, and why? How does the local government justify the collection of taxes? To finance development? How does it deal with challenges to its reasoning?

b. How much does the local structure depend on one group for its existence? What effects does this have on the political structure and culture?

9. Why are supports necessary? What is the relationship between the demands of one group and the support which it gives to the structure?

10. What is the policy of the local government toward the central government? What are the differences between verbal and actual policy? Is independence of action valued? How successful is the local government in presenting its own special needs to the central government?

## C. Future Possibilities

The following questions are concerned with local political trends:

1. How will the local political structure change over time?

a. What will be the future of each of the political parties?

b. How will the power of the executive branch of the local structure change over the next year? Why?

c. How will the fortunes of the local officials, members of the party bureaucracy, businessmen, and others of the 'middle' class change in the next year? Why? What will their reactions be?

d. What interest groups will decline in importance? How will local student groups affect the future of the locality? Local religious groups? How will anticipated changes in the local economy influence the political structure next year? What are the prospects for the radical left?

e. What reforms are on the horizon? Why? With what effects?

f. What new local ordinances relating to politics are likely? What is the future of the political sanctions?

g. What is the future role of corruption in the local bureaucracy?

h. What local personalities might be removed from the scene due to death, assassination, coup, or political defeat? What will the consequences be? What new personalities are emerging?

i. What will be the issues in the next local campaign? Why? How have they changed over the last year?

2. What changes are likely in values and attitudes?

a. What will the effect of increased contact with Western ideas be? Through what channels will this contact take place? Will political attitudes change? How will these changes affect the political structure and process? Political demands and supports?

b. What new values might arise in the near future in this area (e.g. security, preservation of local culture, self-reliance)? Judge the effects these new values will have on the political process and the political structure.

c. Can a class awareness develop? Why or why not? What would be the consequences? Can a minority group develop its own group awareness? What would be the likely consequences?

d. What new policies in the educational realm might have an impact on local politics?

3. What changes are likely in the political process?

a. How will the form of demands change? Will they be more violent? How will this affect the way the government responds?

b. What types of changes do you foresee in the kinds of campaigns waged? The issues raised?

c. Will intellectuals in the community become more or less involved in the political process? If less, will this lead to alienation? If more, will this lead to conflict? In any case, what will the consequences be?

d. What new financial supports might the government seek and find? Will taxes be raised, lowered, or eliminated for some groups?

e. Will funding from the central government continue in its present form? What would be the consequences of increased or decreased funding?

f. From what interest groups will the political structure need support in the near future? How will it cultivate that support? What new interest groups may be forming? What will be the effects of such new interest groups on the political balance?

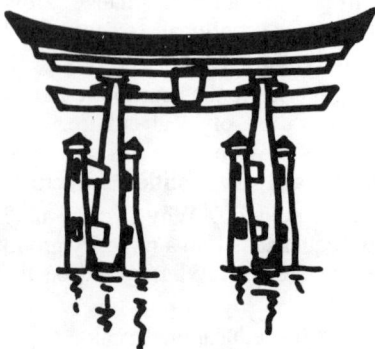

## III. ANOTHER VIEW

The preceding questions seem to presuppose the existence of a powerful, smoothly functioning, clearly defined, and very *visible* government. In many countries, however, the government is quite visible only in the large cities, and at border crossings. Such a government may in fact have a great deal of difficulty mobilizing the active support of its people, and in implementing its programs and regulations. This is particularly true in countries where most of the people are engaged in subsistence agriculture, and where there are numerous different ethnic groups which live in separate regions.

Gunnar Myrdal characterizes such a government as a *soft state*. This implies that although the national government may be able to force compliance with its regulations in any particular case, by and large enforcement is irregular, and village-level awareness of and compliance with national legislation is very low. In such instances, traditional customs and sanctions (often of a religious nature) may in fact be far more important manifestations of a kind of autonomously-functioning 'local government.'

To come to understand a *soft state*, it would be important to discover what in fact are the practical limits to state power, and why these limits exist. Is the state really representing the interests of the peasants, in their eyes? Are members of the national government seen by the peasants as power usurpers living in a distant city, leading lives far removed from that of the peasantry?

Some of the questions in the preceding section can aid in understanding the *soft state*, but another fruitful line of inquiry would be to try to understand the relationship of the average individual to the state. Does the state limit his/her activities in any way? Can he/she really expect anything from the state, and if so, what are these things? Certainly, imaginative inquiry is required if such a very different political environment is to be understood. Some of the following questions may be useful in such an endeavor:

## A. The State and the Individual; General Questions

1. To what extent do the village people feel the **presence** of the government? In what ways (e.g. through taxes; agricultural extension services; presence of the military, police, or government bureaucrats from outside the area; military conscription; or government price regulation of basic foodstuffs)?

2. What segment of the population belongs to civic organizations and participates in community affairs?

3. How much power do village leaders really have, and how much of their function is purely ceremonial?

4. Are the people more actively interested in local, national, or international affairs?

5. Does there seem to be a **dialogue** between the people and the government?

6. Are people reluctant to *talk politics*?

7. Are animated political discussions held in the hom ?
Elsewhere? Often? Do women participate in them? Wh t
is the content of such discussions? Are there any taboo
topics?

8. Are young people interested in politics? International
affairs?

9. If *you* feel that the poor agricultural workers are
exploited, do *they* seem aware of this exploitation?
a. Do they hold particular people or institutions
accountable for their circumstances? Does their understanding include an international perspective on their
situation?
b. If these people are mobilized to political action, what
form does it take? What values is this action based upon?
Are the goals primarily restorative or transformative?

---

**I conceive that land
belongs to a vast family
of which many are dead,
few are living,
and countless members are still unborn.**

**--Nigerian Tribesman**

---

10. Eric Wolf, who has studied peasant movements in
cross-cultural perspective, claims that often '...*the
peasant utopia is the free village...devoid of tax
collectors, government officials, and large landowners...the peasant is a natural anarchist...*'Comment.

11. Demonstrations in the *soft state* may have a larger
component of political *action* than political *statement*. Is
there a tradition of demonstrations, in the city or in the
rural areas? To what extent are these viewed as a threat
to the authorities? What is the latter's response?

12. If this country is a former colony, do you notice any

remaining traces of feelings of subservience or inferiority vis-a-vis Westerners? In what ways is this manifested? What helps to perpetuate this?

13. Has independence reversed the negative effects of colonialism, or is the country still obviously feeling them? What do you feel is the present moral responsibility of the former colonialists?

## B. Corruption

1. How is *corruption* defined by the local people?

2. How do low civil service salaries affect corruption?

3. What practices (e.g. nepotism) are not considered manifestations of corruption, but rather extensions of traditional obligations to extended-family members? What other practices are not considered *corrupt*, that would be called *corrupt* in the context of your own country? What are the origins of these practices? Are there any practices that are labeled *corrupt* here, but not in your own country? Why?

4. Some writers argue that the importance of corruption in government is not in its *immorality* and the resulting loss of respect for the government. Rather, they say that corruption is a key problem because it weakens the ability of the government to implement its own legislation, and provide services impartially to all of those for whom they are intended. Comment.

---

**People can develop
without more electricity
They cannot develop
without real participation
in decision-making.
—Impact**

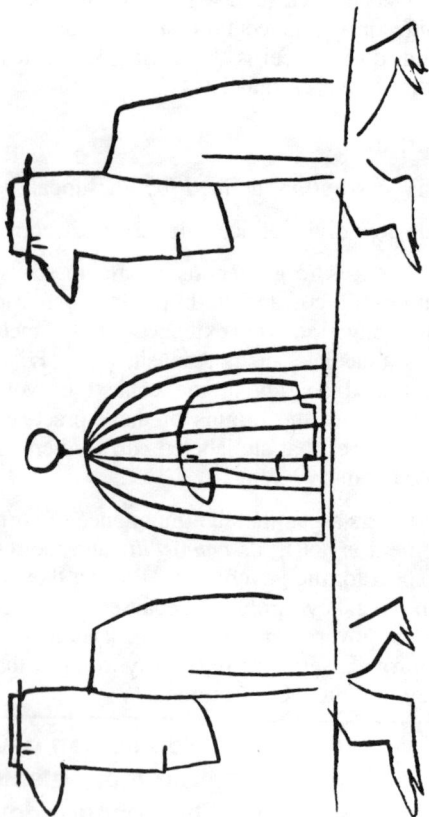

*Some think the peasant is politically immature*

# Social Structure

The fundamental unit of Western society, the nuclear family, shapes our needs differently from those brought up in a non-Western society, where the family structure is 'linear' or 'extended.'

—Joan Tully

# Social Structure

The questions below suggest some of the sociological issues one should be aware of before studying any society, and the broad national problems which are the background of any specific study. The answers to some of these questions can be found in studies already published. The answers to others are either unknown or can never be known finally, because social change makes these answers accurate only for a brief period. Admittedly, many of these questions cannot be answered fully, but they indicate the kinds of basic conditions which affect the individual on the many levels of social interaction.

## A. The National Social Structure

1. What are the basic **class divisions** in the country? What is the history of the class system? Is there a traditional hereditary class structure? Does that structure have some economic, social, religious, or political basis? Is it decaying? Is it being challenged or altered either by social conditions or a new social ideology? Who defends it? Who opposes it? What are the social, economic, political, or ideological reasons for its decay? Is there presently a dual class system, i.e., traditional and modern existing side by side? What kinds of privilege and deferential treatment are accorded the elite in each system? To what extent do the two overlap?

2. Are there **ethnic divisions** within the society? How do these correspond to cultural and linguistic divisions within the country? Are there further subdivisions within the larger groups? Is there a vertical class structure within horizontal groupings (whether of ethnic or other origins)? Are the ethnic divisions related to religious

divisions? What is the political or economic significance of ethnic or religious social divisions?

3. What is the **economic basis of class** in this country? Is it occupation? Income? Living standard? Land ownership? Is conspicuous consumption an important indicator of class?

4. Are there differences between class and social status? Is it possible to have a high income and yet relatively low status or the reverse? How is class related to political influence? How is status related to political influence?

5. Does **dress** reflect social or economic status? Do school children wear uniforms? Why?

6. Do neighborhoods have members of different social classes living near each other? What are the physical boundaries between classes? What linkages exist?

7. What is the nature of **social mobility** in this country? Is there mobility within classes? That is, is it possible to change jobs or places of residence and still remain within the same class? Is there mobility between classes (vertical mobility)? What are the rates and potentials for mobility, both up and down? What are the causes of mobility--education, change in income, change in occupation, politics, religion? When an individual reaches a position of some influence, does this lead to jobs and/or increased status for the members of his/her extended family?

8. Are there separate class hierarchies for men and women? If not, is class a function of the activities or income of the male, the female, or both?

9. How has the experience of **colonialism** or foreign domination affected class structure? Have the upper classes tended to take on the characteristics of their former colonizers? Where do you as a newly-arrived foreigner fit into the class structure? Do you receive special treatment that other strangers do not receive? Why?

10. Is there a city-country status difference? How do the two groups perceive each other? Are there ethnic groups divided along these lines?

---

**Those who benefit from social injustice are naturally less capable of understanding its real character than those who suffer from it.**

**—Reinhold Niebuhr**

---

11. Is there **inter-group friction** based on race, religion, ethnic differences, territoriality, peasant/townsman differences, or labor/management differences? Are the ruling elite characterized by any of these categories, i.e., mainly of one religion or from a particular area? Is there hostility? How is it demonstrated? Is there residential segregation? Forced or voluntary? Is there discrimination in public services or civil rights (e.g. availability of loans or health care)? Is there discrimination in voluntary organizations or informal groups? Do the victims of discrimination have ties to the land? Are they new arrivals? Are there government attempts to eliminate discrimination? In what ways?

12. From your own observations and experiences, describe some of the variations of values and norms between social groups within the local culture.

**Warning!** Class may be the source of social tension. Beware of offending people by asking questions about income or status of certain occupations. Be careful of arousing or uncovering political, religious, or ethnic tensions. Governments and individuals may look rather unfavorably upon you.

Study problems! Remember that there is or may be a great deal of difference between subjective and objective estimations of class. A person may think he is in one class and yet, according to the criteria of the society, be in a different one. Try to find out if an individual uses one criterion for determining his own class and a different criterion for determining his neighbor's class.

A most important requirement for any sociological study is a precise definition of what you are calling *class*. Your first few months of observations might focus on an analysis of what you consider to be the class divisions in your country as compared to the local conceptions of those divisions.

## B. Society and the Individual: City, Town, or Village

The heading for this section suggests a particular perspective for study, that is society and social structure as they affect the single individual. However, one should not feel restricted to this if the resources are available for undertaking a study from a different perspective. Remember that in most of the world, much decision-making and other activities take place on the level of small groups, rather than the level of the individual.

1.a. What are the **occupational groups** in your locality? What are the income levels of these groups? How does occupation and income relate to housing patterns? Which are the choice residential areas of the community? Which areas are overcrowded? How do occupation and income relate to social groupings (friends, people one would see off the job, etc.)?
b. Do villages as units have particular economic activities/specializations?

2. What is the **educational level** of different class or status groups? What are the educational expectations of children of families within those groups? Is the quality, type, and level of education an individual receives related to his ethnic, cultural, or religious background? Does the educational system operate to intensify or

mediate the status and class divisions within the society? Are educated people simply absorbed into the upper classes, thereby cutting off connections with their former peers?

---

**The educational advantages which privilege buys, and the opportunities for the exercise of authority which come with privileged social position, develop capacities which are easily attributed to innate endowment...it has always been the habit of privileged groups to deny the oppressed classes every opportunity for the cultivation of innate capacities and then to accuse them of lacking what they have been denied the right to acquire.**

**--Reinhold Niebuhr**

---

3. Level of **political activity**: What do people classify as political activities? What percentage of each class or social group can be expected to engage in political activities? How often? Are there elections? What groups of people vote? What political groups or candidates are associated with what social or class groups?

4. **Associations**: These can be formal or informal, and are often multifunctional (e.g. an Islamic social welfare organization). What kinds of organizations are most common? Most prestigious? Most influential? Most active? What kinds of people (age, sex, economic class, educational level) compose the memberships of these associations? Are there existing rivalries between different organizations? Do such rivalries appear to be productive or destructive? What are some of the latent functions of these associations?

5. **Recreation**: What are the important leisure time activities? For adults? For children? What is the relative importance of TV, radio, movies, cardplaying, relaxed conversation, outdoor sports (participation and observation), informal visits, musical and dramatic events, etc.? Which population groups participate most heavily in each of these? How does the local concept of *leisure* compare with your own?

6. Is there much movement in and out of the city, of individuals? Of groups? How are new members of the community viewed?

## C. Family and the Individual

This area will probably afford the greatest possibilities for learning and study but will also require the greatest amount of tact and sensitivity. Be aware of male and female role differentiation, and aspects and problems of child-rearing.

1. What is the average **size of families**? Is this increasing or decreasing? What is the average household size? Does the household include grandparents? Aunts, uncles, and their children? Others?

2. Is there a national **family planning** program? How old is the program? How successful is it? Which characteristics of the culture seem to act as barriers to family planning? Which ones facilitate it? Describe the various approaches that the family planning workers are using. Are there economic reasons behind resistance to family planning (e.g. more hands in the fields, security in old age if more children survive, etc.)?    (See *Family Planning* under *HEALTH*)

3. What are the **social relationships within households** and families? Who is the head of the household? What is the role of women within the household? Male children? Female children? The aged? How are decisions which affect the entire family made? Who handles economic

matters dealing with the family or household? Who controls the rearing and socialization of children? What are the priorities of a family (e.g. number of children, income, material possessions, kind of housing, social status, or physical well-being desired)?

4. What constitutes a *good* husband, wife, son, daughter? How much independence do young people have? At what age are they considered adults?

---

**The fundamental unit of Western society, the nuclear family, shapes our needs differently from those brought up in a non-Western society, where the family structure is 'linear' or 'extended.' The extended family meets needs for security and belongingness and personal identity; in the West, people look outside the nuclear family, to institutions such as the government, or to the symbolic value of material things to fulfill needs for security, belongingness, and personal identity.**

**--Joan Tully**

---

5. At what age do children marry? How do **marriages** come about? Who arranges and/or pays for a wedding ceremony? Are they costly? What role do parents play in selecting spouses for their children? Do newly-married couples form new households? What is the expectation or possibility that children will move away from the area in which they were raised, after marriage? What relationship do two married people have with their parents?

6. What is the frequency of **divorce**? What government and religious regulations affect a divorce? What rights do women have under these regulations?

7. The average family in the U.S. remains in one household for a period of 3-4 years. In this country?

8. Are there helpers or servants? Are they generally relatives? How are they regarded and treated? What seems to be the nature of their social, economic, and personal relationships with those for whom they work?

9. What are the important **social customs** of the society? Describe table manners, forms of greeting and their social significance, manners and customs between men and women, expressions of deference and respect, etc. What are the origins and meanings of these customs? How do they relate to class or role differentiation?

## D.   General Questions

1. **Influence patterns**: Who would people go to for advice or help with different problems? Economic problems? Emotional problems? Religious questions? Political questions?

2. Collect data on class divisions and composition within religious and ethnic groups; analyze that data in terms of economic and political power.

3. Compare the family organization and deference patterns between families in different classes.

4. Study the class **roles and associations of foreigners**. This could be done from the viewpoint of the foreigner and also from that of the national.

5. Analyze the class and status of one individual. Describe the factors which determine his social position. Explain how these factors fit into the social structure as a whole.

6. What seem to be the most fundamental problems of the society? What seem to be their causes? Are they perhaps simply symptoms of larger changes taking place?

7. What part does **planning** play in the everyday life of the people?

8. What roles exist for **handicapped** people? How are they treated by others? Why?

9. How does the structure and pace of city life compare with that of city life in the U.S.?

# Roles of Women and Men

What we urgently need is a change
in the attitudes of both men and women,
solidarity among all women,
and a new kind of partnership
between men and women.
Only then can we hope to achieve
the goals we have set ourselves.

--Helvi Sipila, United Nations

# Roles of
# Women and Men

## A. Rearing and Socialization of Children

1. Are female and male children equally valued and accepted? Are they treated equally in the home? Do they share equally in chores, punishments, and privileges?

2. Do the sexes mix socially? If not, what activities seem to attract each? How do girls relate to one another? What topics do they discuss? What physical intimacies are they allowed? Ask the same questions for boys. How do young girls and young boys relate to each other? How do they relate to male and female adults in the home and neighborhood?

3. What ritual **ceremonies** are there for girls? For boys? How do they differ?

4. What adults are to be found in the community to serve as **models** for young girls? For young boys?

5. What **psychological traits** are associated with women? With men? How are these traits valued by the society?

## B. Marriage and Child-rearing

1. How much emphasis is placed on marriage for women? For men? How are marriages decided upon? What are courting and/or selection procedures? Is there a dowry? Is it token or substantial relative to the cost of living? Is it status-oriented?

2. Whose **extended family** does the newly-married couple become part of? Who is the head of the house-

hold? Are family decisions made by one partner, or both? What are the roles of men and women in family economic, or discipline matters? What are the responsibilities of each of the partners in the marriage and family? How much control does each have over his/her children's lives, his/her mate's life, and his/her own life?

3. How strong is **religion** in defining marriage roles? Are inter-religious marriages possible? Under what conditions? May either husband or wife have more than one spouse? Under what conditions? What are the rights of women and men in marriages and divorces?

4. How many children does the average woman have? What part do the father and mother each play in rearing or socializing children? Is child-rearing handled communally or on a parent-child basis? Are birth-control methods and devices known and available? Is their use generally accepted? What roles do older people play (grandparents, aunts and uncles) in extended families?

## C. Economic Considerations

1. What are the inheritance laws of the society? Who owns **property**? Are mates considered property? Do men adorn women with gifts of value, or vice versa?

---

**In all countries women play a large role in production for family use. Since a large share of those family activities which decline and disappear in the process of development are women's work within the family, the problem of women's reaction to this change is of crucial importance for the scope and pattern of development... When families gradually change over to use part of the cash income earned by male family members to purchase products which the women had hitherto produced, important changes in the women's position and outlook must occur.**

**--Ester Boserup**

---

2. What are the **occupational patterns** for both men and women? What is the nature of outside work--domestic, manufacturing, administrative? Are women and men paid equally when doing similar jobs? Do they have equal upward mobility? Do married people operate business enterprises independently of their spouses? Are there economic activities that are almost exclusively controlled by either men or women (e.g. marketing, animal-raising, or textile production)?

3. What **medical facilities** are there for child-birth, birth-control, women's health, etc.?

4. Is female or male **prostitution** widespread? What is

the social acceptance or defined role of prostitutes in the community? How does the image of male prostitutes compare with that of female prostitutes?

## D. In the Community

1. What are the roles of men and women in their local communities? At larger social and governmental levels? Are both men and women employed in all levels of government?

2. Do both men and women participate in the arts? Which arts? What is the nature of their participation? How are women and men portrayed in literature, history, and drama?

3. What role do women and men play in religious matters on a local level? Are there religious constraints that are particularly directed toward either sex (e.g. regarding menstrual periods or childbirth)? Do both women and men participate in ceremonies? How do their roles differ?

4. What are the other interests and/or pastimes of adult women and men?

# Religion and Beliefs

It makes a great deal of difference
whether you call life
a dream, a pilgrimage, a labyrinth,
or a carnival.

—Kenneth Burke

# Religion and Beliefs

Drawing the line between religious and other beliefs is difficult. In any culture, some people do not subscribe to any religion. Such 'non-believers' may constitute a substantial percentage of the population. Certainly all societies maintain important beliefs not usually classified as *religious*. The following questions, with minor adaptations, can be directed towards beliefs of all kinds, and the organizations, groups, and systems focused around them.

## A. Membership and Organization

1. What **religions** are practiced in the country?

a. What proportion of the people are followers of each religion? Is one of the religions dominant or designated the national religion? Do any of the religious sects have only a small number of followers?

b. Are followers of the different religions accepting of each other? How are those who follow a minority religion treated? Are they regarded as socially deviant? If there is persecution, how is it manifested?

2. Who are the **followers** of each religion?

a. Does a particular religion appeal to a particular ethnic group, social class, or geographic area? Why?

b. Are there role or status differences based on sex within any religion?

c. How does the level of commitment among members vary? What are the different forms and degrees of participation?

d. How are new members recruited? Are there restrictions? What are the requirements?

e. Are there major divisions within the religious communities for ideological or other reasons?

## 3. How are the religions **organized**?

a. Are there definite hierarchies? What are the positions of leadership? What are the leaders' responsibilities? How do they relate to the rest of the members of their own religion, and to those outside of it?

b. Who are the leaders? What are their ethnic, geographic, social, and educational backgrounds? Compare them with other followers of the religion and the populace as a whole? What positions do they hold in the secular society? What kind of training and screening do these religious authorities undergo? Is there a shared viewpoint towards not only religious, but also social, political, and cultural issues? Are the leaders isolated from the community they work in? Do they follow particular lifestyles? Are both men and women in positions of leadership?

---

**...whatever universality a given religious tradition manages to attain arises from its ability to engage a widening set of individual, even idiosyncratic, conceptions of life and yet somehow sustain and elaborate them all.**

**--Clifford Geertz**

---

c. What are the local organizations of members (e.g. church congregations or neighborhood temples)? On what basis are these formed (e.g. proximity, familial ties, agreement on controversial issues, social or religious classes)? What areas do they serve? What are the relations among these local organizations and with district or national level administration? What are the relations with the government on all levels?

d. What role does the family play in religious affairs?

e. Are the religious organizations doing well financially? How are they financed?

f. How do the organizations of the various religions compare?

## B. Beliefs and Practices

1. Is there a structure or system to the **beliefs** of each of the religions? What are those ideologies?

a. What are the beliefs concerning a god, gods, or other deities? Do ancestors play an important role in the religious beliefs? What household gods or spirits are part of the beliefs?

b. How are questions such as the following answered: What is the origin of the world? Does it have an ultimate design or 'purpose? What is real and what is illusory? What should people base their knowledge and judgements on? How does one know what is true? What is the relation of a person to nature, to his or her god(s), to other people, and to him or herself? What are the characteristics of the *good* person? What is *human nature*? What is the *good life*?

c. What is the preferred orientation: *doing, being, becoming*? What is the time orientation?

d. What ethical beliefs are held?

e. Focus on some key concepts and values. What are the attitudes towards: *freedom, responsibility, obligation, authority, progress, success, community, individualism, privacy, status, role, efficiency, property, materialism, friendship, masculinity,* and *femininity*?

f. Who arbitrates differences in opinion, or clarifies teachings? Who is the final authority on ideological matters?

g. How are the beliefs integrated? From your own personal point of view, what are the seeming contradictions or inconsistencies, if any?

h. Compare the ideologies of the various religions. What sets them apart from one another?

i. Describe some of the variations of values and norms between social groups within the country.

---

**Is not religion
all deeds and all reflection,
and that which is neither
deed nor reflection
but a wonder and a surprise
ever springing in the soul,
even while the hands hew the stone
or tend the loom?**

**—Kahlil Gibran**

---

2. What are the religious **practices**? Compare them with the ideologies. How are the systems of beliefs expressed? How are they reaffirmed by the authorities? By laymen?

a. What are the regular meetings, services, or rituals? Where do these take place?

b. What is the religious calendar like? What ceremonies or festivals are celebrated or performed? Where do they take place? What significance do they have? What proportion of the population participates? Describe the events.

c. What are the duties of the leaders?

d. How are the various rites of passage (e.g. birth, marriage, death) acknowledged and commemorated?

e. What seemingly functional practices (e.g. bathing,

rising in the morning) take on special religious significance?

f. What are the behavior expectations within sacred places or during rituals? How do they compare with expectations elsewhere? What kinds of dietary laws or other religious taboos exist? What incentives or sanctions are used to encourage or enforce proper behavior?

g. Compare the practices of the various religions. How do they differ?

3. What are the **beliefs or practices outside** of any of the organized religions in the country?

a. What beliefs, if any, from major religions other than those practiced in the country are held? How has this happened (e.g. diffusion from another culture, historical roots that still persist)?

b. What *folk beliefs* or indigenous practices of the country exist which are independent of the established religions? What are the superstitions or myths? What system or pattern to these beliefs exists? How did such beliefs evolve?

c. What folk derivations or modifications of the established religions exist? Are they disapproved of by the authorities?

d. How pervasive is the influence of these beliefs outside of the established religions? Are they held by all the classes or are there different superstitions and myths for different groups? What social function do they serve in the community? Do conflicts arise between either the beliefs from other religions or the folk beliefs and the established religions?

## C. Religious Expression

1. What buildings and structures, tools, implements, and **materials** are used in the religious practices?

a. How are the buildings and structures used? Are they considered sacred places? Who can enter or utilize these structures?

b. Are monuments, altars, or statues of religious importance erected?

c. Are offerings made? What is offered? How? For what or whom? When? Where? Why?

d. Who uses the religious implements and who creates the offerings?

e. What are the rules of dress according to religious prescriptions, for everyday and special occasions? Do leaders wear special clothing or ornaments?

f. How do all of the above act as symbols?

2. What kinds of **writings**, documents, and myths have been important to the followers of the religions?

a. In what ways do they exhort, persuade, or compel readers to follow their prescriptions and codes? What literary forms do the writings take (e.g. stories, parables, aphorisms)? How do the followers of the religions interpret the writings? How do the religious authorities interpret them? How have these writings influenced the secular literature of the country?

b. Are there epics in the chronicles of the religions? What part do they play in the cultural identity of the people? How do they compare with the evolution of the people as historians have written about it? How do they relate to the demands made upon individuals in everyday life?

c. What myths are widely held? What do they say about the basic assumptions on which local cultural values and beliefs are based? Are the myths still *alive*, or have they been reduced to mere stories?

d. If you know the language, look at words and phrases (e.g. commonly used metaphors) that have religious connotations or derivations, and relate them to the context in which they are used.

3. What kinds of religious **music and art** are produced?

a. Is the art sacred or descriptive? Who is allowed to create the objects? What kinds of materials are used? What styles are used? When, how, where, and for what purpose is the art displayed? How do these things reflect the religious beliefs? How do the works of art function as symbols?

b. Consider the above questions with regard to religious music.

c. How do religious art and music relate to everyday life? Compare them to secular art and music and trace the influences of each upon the other. How do the art and music reflect the viewpoints of the artists? How do they reflect the viewpoints of the religious authorities?

---

**There are various ways in which faith unites man's mental life and gives it a dominating center. It can be the way of discipline which regulates daily life; it can be the way of meditation and contemplation; it can be the way of concentration on the ordinary work, or on a special aim or on another human being.**

**--Paul Tillich**

---

## D. Religion and the Community

1. How important are the religions as **cultural forces**?

a. How do the religions under study fit into the local life of the community? Look at different social classes.

b. How much and how well do the religions provide guidance to the lay person? Do they constitute a means of social control? How and to what extent are religious principles realized in the social practices of the community? Is there widespread acceptance of some practices that run counter to the religious principles?

c. The word *religion* comes from the Latin *religare*, 'to bind together.' Do the ideologies of the religions do that for the community?

2. How active are the religious organizations in **community affairs**?

a. Do they provide welfare services for the community? What roles do religious leaders play in counseling and in community projects?

b. Do they have any influence on public education? Do they run their own schools?

3. What are the positions of the religious organizations on political issues?

a. Do they tend to support or undermine the status quo? What are their postions on social change? How do they view the social structure of the community? Do they recognize the need for economic reforms and an improvement in living conditions for the lower classes?

b. What stands do these organizations take on ethical issues facing the country (e.g. definition and punishment of crimes, policies towards minority groups, war)?

c. How do the religious organizations influence governmental legislation? What reforms, if any, have been urged on the government? What reaction do these organizations seem to recommend in the face of injustice (e.g. active opposition, acceptance, transcendence)?

## E.  History and Change

1. Trace the evolution of the religions. How did they

come to be practiced in this country? To what extent are the religions indigenous faiths? Are there indications of origins in other religions or local folk practices?

2. How have the religions affected the political and social trends? How have they influenced art, music, literature, drama, etc.?

3. Are the religions increasing or decreasing in importance as a cultural force?

a. Do they recognize the need for change within themselves? How are rituals changing to become more relevant to the life of the people of all levels of society?

b. Is the feeling of community among the people who practice a common religion changing with modernization? Is there a general trend towards secularization?

c. What are the future prospects for the various religions?

## F. Influence of Foreign Religions

1. Compare the forms of the religions found in this country with forms found in other countries. What is their historical relationship? Do they have formal or informal ties on an international basis at the present time? Do religiously oriented international service organizations operate in the country?

2. Are there missionaries present in the community? How are they viewed by community members and by the national government? What are their goals (e.g. conversion, education, communication, service)? Are they accepting of other religions? Whom do they seek as new members?

3. Compare and contrast beliefs, values, and concepts of this country with those of others, and in particular with those of your own country.

# Music and Art

Being an artist means
not reckoning and counting
but ripening, like the tree
that does not force its sap.

—Rainer Maria Rilke

# Music and Art

## A. Music

1. What are the different uses of the human **voice** in music? Is singing common? Consider uses other than melody line singing also. What kinds of sounds are produced beyond the purely tonal (e.g. chants, grunts to produce rhythms, falsetto, nasal tones)? How are the different voices of men, women, and children utilized?

2. Describe the various **instruments** used in producing the musical system under study. Can you trace their evolution from earlier, cruder instruments? How are the instruments made? What influence has the improvement in techniques of construction had over time? What is the tonal quality of the instrument you are studying? What is the technique required?

3. What are the various **types of music**? Is there religious music? Is there a distinction between *folk music*, and *court music* or music of a particular class? What are the different trends within the types of music? How does the type of music vary with the locale?

4. Analyze a particular **musical system.** Because non-Western music should not be judged by Western criteria, full attention should be paid to distinctions between Western conceptions and the full range of musical possibilities. For example, the musical system under consideration may be anharmonic, contain isotonic scales, be melodically heterophonic, or involve rhythmic complications and unusual melody types dictated by religious or secular traditions.

a. **Scales**--Does the musical system have a composite scale from which tones are drawn to make up the use scale of a particular song? How many tones are in that scale? What is the smallest interval between tones? Are these divisions regular? What are the factors that might influence the selection of tones used in forming scales (e.g. relations to overtones, equal intervals between tones, consonance, extramusical factors such as the construction of some instrument, religious prescriptions, or tonal intervals from nature such as the singing of birds)? If a scale cannot be determined, consider some of the problems encountered in trying to analyze the scale (i.e. modulation or the transfer of motives to different pitch levels, the frequent use of ornamental notes, the absence of anything corresponding to a tonic or final).

b. **Rhythm**--What are the standard rhythms? What factors influence the choice of rhythm? Is there a relation between rhythm and meter in the composition under study? Describe that relation taking into account rhythmic differences from Western music such as the use of syncopation effects, accentuation of weak beats, counter rhythms produced by percussion instruments against the melodic rhythms. If the composition defies the traditional concept of meter, detail why this is so.

c. **Melody**--Consider the size, direction, frequency, initial and cadence characteristics, and relation to motive and phrase structure of the intervals used in the melody. What kinds of motive structures are employed? How is repetition utilized? Are musical pieces divided into rhythmic or melodic units? How is a new unit introduced? Discuss the rhythmic pattern of the melody and how it relates to the motive structure. Elaborate on the expression characteristics of the melody as a whole, utilizing whatever background information on the composition and lyrics is available.

d. **Harmony**--Is the musical system essentially homophonic, heterophonic, or polyphonic? If polyphonic, what are the constituent parts? Do contrapuntal harmonies exist? What is the relative importance of chords versus independent melodies?

5. What are the settings for **performance**? Does the music accompany other activities such as drama, ceremonies, dances, or parties?

## B. Art

1. What **forms** does art take?

2. In **painting** and **drawing**, what mediums are used? What are the artist's techniques and how does he or she use them? Discuss composition, size, direction, perspective, motion, color, light.

3. In **sculpture**, what materials and tools are used? What is the relationship of materials to specific form? Why was a particular material chosen? What is the material's influence on the appeal of the work? What is the influence of form in one material on forms in other materials? What methods are employed (e.g. additive modeling, subtractive modeling)? As for painting and drawing, discuss the expressive elements of sculpture.

4. What materials and tools are used in the production of **ceramics**? What are the forms? What are the types of decoration? Discuss the expressive elements.

5. Consider other art forms such as rare books, cal-

ligraphy, printing, weaving, etc. What importance in comparison and relationship to other art forms do they have? Why are they considered art in this culture? What are the techniques and materials of the artist? Discuss the expressive elements.

6. Can any of the following terms be applied to the art of this culture: *representative, symbolic, impressionistic*? If the art is *representative*, what is represented? Are definite likenesses of natural forms created? Do the forms represent other forms? Is the art ever abstract? How is the order attained in the works of art? To what extent is lack of order expressive for the artist?

7. Is art **displayed**? How and in what settings? For whom?

## C. Architecture

1. What is the **purpose** of the structure? How does the structure succeed or fail in fulfilling its purpose?

2. What **materials** are used? How? Why? How do the architect's tools and resources affect his or her product? What is the influence of the climate on the structure?

3. What architectural **shapes** are employed? How does the architect deal with mass, space, light, air, etc.? What is the relationship of the exterior to the interior?

4. How does the architect deal with **social problems** of economy and human use? Ecological considerations?

## D. Questions Relating To All The Arts

1. Who are the artists and musicians? Are they professionals? What is there social status? Is it more likely for one of the sexes or a particular social or economic class to become an artist or musician? What are the important positions, the leadership roles? What is the relation of the artist or musician to others? How is the artist or musician trained? Are art and music taught in the public

schools? Do parents instruct their children? What are some of the attitudes of the artist or musician towards his or her work?

2.  How do the artist and the musician **create**? What kind of planning goes into the work? Are models (the work of accepted masters) followed, or does the artist/musician strive for originality? Relate this to art and the society as a whole.

3.  What are the basic purposes of art and music in this culture?

a.  Is accurate representation of the world a purpose? Is the artist an impartial chronicler of physical reality? Is a personal interpretation of reality sought? Does the artist comment on reality? Does he seek to add a part of his own insight into the work? Is convention sought? Does the artist accept certain basic standards of representation that are traditional? If so, what is this tradition, how did it evolve, what changes has it undergone, and how does it derive its justification? Within the tradition, how does an individual artist express his individuality?

b.  Is the creation of beauty, both in the content of the work and in the physical form a purpose? If this is so, discuss the basic components of beauty in this art.

c.  Is the expression of inward experience the purpose? If so, is it through dramatic representation of situations which arouse feelings? Is it through manipulation of light, color, form, or other technical factors, while still representing something of reality? Is it through non-representational forms of light, color, and form? Is it through choice of subject matter?

d.  Does the art or music of this culture have religious purposes?

e.  Does the art or music of this culture have political purposes?

4.  Who is the art and music intended for (e.g. the artists themselves, the general public, an intellectual or artistic elite)? Who appreciates the art and music? What are the reactions inspired or provoked?

5.  Who judges what is good and what criteria are used? Are art and music relative only to personal taste? Are they relative to cultural tastes, that is, does the quality of the work depend on the way it interprets the aims and needs of the specific culture? Are they relative to 'eternal laws' and if so, who has established these 'laws'? Are they judged by their functionality, their human usefulness? Are they judged by their concern with basic human problems and needs? Must they be profound to be 'good'? Are they judged by how well they communicate their messages?

6.  What has been the **history** or development of art and music in this culture? Consider a particular medium or school of art or music. Consider art and music as a whole and the influences of the various media and schools on each other.

7.  What have been and continue to be the **external influences** on art and music?

a.  How does the cultural environment affect art and

music? Are the arts socially stratified?

b. How does the physical environment affect art and music?

c. What is the role of the government in promoting or restricting art and music? How are they affected by the economic system?

d. How do religions influence the art and music of this culture?

e. What political, social, cultural, and religious changes in history have provoked changes in the art and music? What changes in art have provoked changes in other areas?

f. How have other cultures affected the art and music of this culture? What have been the reverse effects?

# Food

Breaking bread together
gives nourishment to bodies
and friendships.

# Food

1. What are the most important foods in the **diet** of most people? Are any of these imported? Are they canned, frozen, dried, or preserved in some other way? Who does this work?

2. How do the important foods break down into the categories of **protein, fats,** and **carbohydrates**?

3. What is the extent of **meat** and other animal product consumption?

4. Are meat animals raised in special pens? Are they fed or do they forage for their own food?

5. How important are **fish** in the diet? Does this differ greatly between the coastal areas and those farther inland? Are fish raised in ponds or caught through traditional methods?

6. What kinds of **fruits and vegetables** are consumed? Are they seasonal? Which are the most popular? The most expensive?

7. Are there major **vegetable sources of protein** such as soybeans or peanuts?

8. What is the incidence of disorders related to **malnutrition**? (See *Nutrition* under *HEALTH*)

9. What kinds of sweets or desserts exist? Under what circumstances are they eaten?

10. Are spices or herbs used in great quantity or great variety?

11. What are the local **beverages**? Tea, coffee, milk, wine, beer, local fruit drinks? For local alcoholic beverages, describe the production process, storage procedure, and social significance.

12. Are there any occasions/festivals/holidays when large amounts of food are specially prepared and eaten? What foods, and what is the significance of each? Beverages?

13. What kind of food **taboos** are there? Why do they exist? How carefully are they followed? What are the consequences of breaking a food taboo?

14. What products are chewed or smoked, e.g. tobacco, coca leaves, opium, betel nut, etc.? Is this done primarily at gatherings of some sort?

15. What kinds of drinks and foods are served to **guests**? Is there an obligation to do so?

16. What kinds of foods are offered in **restaurants**? Are there status reasons why certain foods are not offered?

17. What kinds of foods are available at **street stalls**? Who buys this food? Why? How does this food differ from that available in most homes, and that available in restaurants? Are such food stalls centers of social activity?

18. To what extent is **cooking** considered an art? A chore?

19. How is cooking knowledge disseminated? Are there **cookbooks** available? Are they widely used? Who does the cooking in the family?

20. What are the most common methods of cooking? What utensils and equipment are used? What kind of fuel sources are used?

21. What percentage of the family **budget** do food and kitchen equipment/operating expenses represent?

22. Is food for an individual household purchased daily? What kinds of storage facilities exist in the home?

23. How many times a day is cooking done? Is it important that food or drinks be served hot (or cold)?

24. Are chopsticks, knives/forks/spoons, or hands used to eat with? Is food eaten in separate courses? On separate plates?

25. What are the rules governing eating away from the home (e.g. no eating allowed on the street, or eating on the street allowed, but not while walking)?

26. Describe the table manners and general food-related social expectations.


See also the questions on agriculture in the section on *ECONOMICS*.

# Education

The first step
in the education of people
is to convince them that
they already know a great deal.

--Paulo Freire

# Education

## A. Structure

1. What are the major **divisions** of the public education system? How many grades are in each division? How many possible channels or tracks?

2. Does national law require a certain number of years of **compulsory** education? How many? What percentage of the population in each age group is in fact enrolled in school? Is compulsory attendance enforced? What is the effect of compulsory schooling in the rural areas?

3. Is the school system **modeled** after that of another country? What country? What effects does this have on the *appropriateness* of the school system with respect to national needs? Are there presently any efforts to redirect the focus of education to fit these needs (e.g. schools of engineering beginning to concentrate on *adapting* technology to fit local circumstances, rather than giving a classical engineering education)?

4. **Types** of schools:

a. Are there many religious schools? What is their impact on society?

b. Are there special schools or programs for vocational training? What are the advantages and disadvantages of such training at the secondary level (as opposed to general education, or apprenticeship programs with factories and shops)?

c. What programs exist for adult education (especially literacy programs), or for *upgrading* particular personnel? How effective are such programs? In what ways, if any, does the school function as a community center? Is there an agricultural extension service?

d. What institutions exist for military education? Are there programs for military instruction in the public universities or high schools? Do military personnel study in other countries?

e. Compare the quality of the various types of schools. Compare urban schools with rural schools.

## B. Administration and Finances

1. To what extent is the educational system under the **centralized** control of the national government? How is the country (or a particular city) divided up into districts? To what extent are schools locally administered?

2. Are school officials appointed or elected? Are there unofficial positions of authority? What roles do parents play?

3. Is the bureaucracy of the national ministry of education large enough and competent enough to administer the school system? Centralized control can be used to foster socio-political integration and to promote development, but it can also lead to neglect of local conditions and needs. What do you see as the advantages and disadvantages of the existing system with respect to centralization?

4. Does the national ministry of education seek to **regulate** private, religious, or commercially-operated schools? In what ways? What is the relative importance of these schools within the larger educational system?

5. How is the public educational system **financed**? What are the national and local budgets?

6. Do students pay **tuition** or entrance fees? If so, how much? Is 'free' education provided for a certain number of years?

7. What are the most pressing needs (e.g. more buildings, better books and equipment, more teachers,

subject matter more relevant to national problems)? How could these needs be met?

## C. Facilities

1. Where are the schools located? What buildings are available? In what condition (age, size, construction materials) are these buildings?

2. What facilities and equipment are available (e.g. classrooms, desks, libraries, lunchrooms, restrooms, science labs, auditoriums, health and physical education facilities, films, and audio-visual equipment)? Which of these, if any, do you think are critical to the learning process, and which are simply supplemental aids? Why?

3. What is the pupil/classroom ratio? Are the facilities adequate?

4. What facilities external to the actual school buildings are used, that are not used in your own country?

5. Consider the above questions for the various divisions and for both public and private schools. What differences exist?

## D. Curriculum

1. What **language(s)** are used for instruction? What language(s) are taught? Beginning at what level?

2. What are the relative emphases of **science and technical knowledge** versus reading/writing skills and social studies (at each level)? Are there classes in art and music (instruction and participation)?

3. To what extent do primary or secondary school curricula in the **rural areas** have a rural agriculture orientation? Does this help to diminish the effect that schools might have in alienating children from their village environment? Does it make it more difficult for village children to move up in the urban schools? How

do the local people view this?

4. Does the curriculum include **religious** instruction? Of what nature? Is it the same for all? Who teaches the religious courses? What is the relative importance of these courses within the curriculum?

5. How much do students know about other countries (especially your country)? How was this knowledge gained? Reflect on this question as it applies to students in your own country.

6. What **extra-curricular** activities are possible?

7. What are the backgrounds of most **teachers**? How are they trained? Is the training sufficient? What is the traditional role of the teacher in the classroom? What is his/her traditional status in the society? Present status?

8. What **teaching techniques** are used?

9. How much are teachers' **salaries**? How do they compare with those of others in both public and private sectors? Are teachers protected by tenure or civil service laws? How high is the rate of turnover?

10. What is the teacher/student ratio?

11. What is a *good student*? How are students promoted? What rewards and punishments are used? What are the standards of attendance, conduct, and performance? How are problems handled?

## E. Orientation

1. What kind of education is valued (e.g. technical, intellectual, artistic, physical, spiritual)?

2. Especially at the primary and secondary levels, to what extent is the curriculum specifically designed for political **socialization**? What attitudes and ideologies are projected?

3. To what extent is the curriculum, especially at the

secondary level, designed to promote positive orientations toward economic **modernization**? Does it encourage positive orientations toward physical labor? Do the schools attempt to teach specific skills which may be used in a modernizing economy?

4. Does the curriculum material seek to create positive attitudes toward individual accomplishment? Does it emphasize group achievement through cooperation? What does it emphasize? What traditional values relate to the above?

---

**The educational system of the colonizers had in fact deeply implanted in the mind of the colonized intellectual the notion that the essential qualities remain eternal inspite of all the blunders men may make: the essential qualities of the West, of course. The native intellectual accepted the cogency of these ideas, and deep down in his brain you could always find a vigilant sentinel ready to defend the Greco-Latin pedestal.**

**—Frantz Fanon**

---

5. To what extent are the structure and curricula of the public educational system designed to meet the projected labor needs for the developing economy? What assumptions are implicit in such planning by the national government?

6. What general knowledge do people have of the various levels of schools? What are the local opinions? Are there differences in the value placed on education by adults and youths?

7. How important is the educational system to the

particular community you are observing?

8. What generalizations can you make about student attitudes and aspirations, especially at the higher levels? Do these students have an elitist orientation? What value do they assign to their schooling?

## F. Historical Background

1. What were the forms and content of institutions in the dominant **traditional** culture which performed educational functions? What were the relationships of these educational institutions to the dominant social hierarchy and to the religious order of the culture?

2. If the nation experienced **colonial** domination, what was the educational policy of the colonial government? Did it build an educational system? If so, on what scale and for what purpose? What impact did education during the colonial period have on the independence movement, post-independence development, and current concepts of education?

3. How has the educational system grown and developed in **recent** times?

## G. Effects

1. The concept of education may include far more than schooling; it may encompass all aspects of enculturation. How do the schools complement or contradict other forces of socialization?

2. Do the local people feel that curriculum should attempt to transmit **traditional** values and norms, or **modern** values and norms, which may not have originated in their culture?

3. What fraction of highly-trained personnel attend **foreign universities**? What do they study? In what countries do they study? What are the arrangements?

What are the pros and cons of overseas education for the educated elite? Does a *brain drain* result? Are there any government regulations that attempt to reduce the brain drain? Are they effectively enforced?

4. Do the schools prepare trained personnel who can make contributions by filling new **economic and technical roles**? What areas of study are most useful from an economic standpoint? To what extent does the educational system, particularly the universities, favor these areas? Do the schools encourage new thinkers, poets, and writers?

---

### Education does not mean extending something from the 'seat of knowledge' to the 'seat of ignorance.'

### --CERES

---

5. Are many educated persons **unemployed** because they cannot find jobs which meet their status expectations? What are the potential political consequences of unemployment among the educated? Is this a temporary lag between growth in education and growth in the economic system, which will correct itself in time?

6. How is public education used to promote political and social **integration**? Is it a useful instrument for creating national loyalties and transmitting the national language? What effect does it have on ethnic and other social divisions within the nation?

7. To what extent does public demand for education constitute a **political pressure** on the government? How well does it meet this demand? Does the government view widespread education as a potentially destabilizing influence?

8. The school system is the primary channel for upward **social mobility** in most developing nations. To what

extent is this true in this country? What structural features of the educational system have an impact on social mobility and stratification? Is education monopolized by the upper and middle classes, and thus does it offer little social opportunity for the lower classes? How could this situation be changed? Are educated members of the lower classes absorbed into the elite, thereby breaking their ties with the lower classes?

9. Is has been argued that developing nations will never have the resources to provide equal educational opportunites for all, and consequently schools can only serve to benefit the upper and middle classes. Do you think this is true in this country? If so, what are the consequences, both present and future? What alternative forms of education (other than schools) could be fruitfully developed?

## H. If You Are A Student Or Teacher

If you are in the country as a teacher or student there are many questions related to classrooms and students that you will be asking yourself. Hopefully a better understanding of students, their classroom behavior, and their circumstances will not only help your teaching or studying but also give you some idea of the general educational setting, and another means of insight into the culture as a whole.

1. What expectations about the **role of the teacher** do students seem to have? How well do you or the teachers fulfill these expectations? What adaptations do the students make to a teacher's behavior? Do you feel that a teacher should try to fulfill the students' expectations? Why or why not?

2. What are the educational histories of the **students**? To what extent do class or ethnic background seem to influence the apparent ability, motivation, classroom behavior, and learning problems of students in the

educational system? (Be cautious about generalizations here.)

3. With what pedagogical **techniques** are students most familiar and comfortable? To what techniques are they most responsive? Are students normally passive, or do they actively participate in discussion? What is done to encourage students to give feedback on teaching techniques?

4. What standards are used to judge your own and others' abilities and effectiveness as teachers or students? Do you observe other teachers? Do they observe you? Are comparisons made? How do you and the others feel about it?

5. How do students feel about competition with each other, grading, and class ranking? How do you feel about these things? How do both of these factors affect your studying or teaching?

6. What are the **cultural** settings, norms, and values projected by the teaching materials available? How appropriate do you feel they are to the actual setting? Do you feel that curriculum material should project traditional settings and norms? *Modern* or *revolutionary* settings and norms?

7. Why do students want to study the subjects that are offered?

8. What subjects are you teaching or studying? Why? Why are you doing so in this particular place?

# Communications

Clasp the hands
and know the thoughts
of men in other lands.
—John Masefield

# Communications

## A. Forms of Communication

1. Which **newspapers and magazines** are most popular? What is their average circulation? Distribution?

2. Which **radio** stations are most popular? Do they have a similar format to those in the U.S.? How do they differ?

3. Is there **television**? What kinds of shows are most popular? How does this compare with TV in the U.S.?

4. What kinds of movies are popular? What audience reaction or behavior do you observe? How frequently do various classes of people attend? Is there advertising? Who is it aimed at?

5. What kinds of **books** are available? What is the relative price? Are there public libraries? Are they free? What are the local people's reading habits? Do these vary with class?

6. Are there any forms of media that are present in your home country, but not in your host country? Why?

7. What forms of communication are utilized that do not exist in your home country (e.g. banners over roads, loudspeaker trucks advertising films, market-place meetings, forms of social theatre)?

## B. Freedoms and Censorship

1. Do the constitution or the laws of the country provide for **freedom of speech** and freedom of the press? If not, what are the constraints? Does the government strictly adhere to its freedom of speech laws?

2. Are there any organizations which are especially concerned with keeping the communications channels free

of barriers to the communication of ideas that are controversial, or which are politically or religiously unorthodox? Are individuals and groups allowed to express unpopular opinions? What limits does freedom of expression have? Do these limits have traditional, cultural roots?

3. What is the **government attitude** towards the media? Is it restrictive, regulatory, participatory, cooperative?

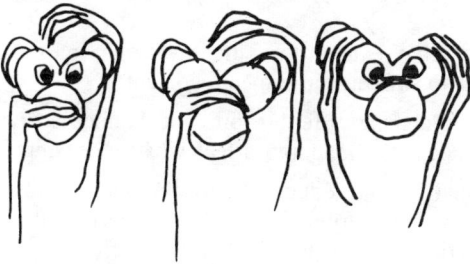

4. *In government censorship, some official or board is empowered to suppress, refuse a license to, or otherwise deal with, certain classes of material, whether they be books, magazines, motion pictures, dramatic productions, or other media of communication.*

--From **Studying Your Community**

This may also extend to refusal to grant permission to use an auditorium for a speech or discussion, and similar actions. What are the laws concerning censorship? What justifications are given? Who are the censors? What do the common people feel about this censorship?

5. Is it legal for the government to take total control of the media in the country? Has this ever occurred?

6. What qualifications must be met before a broadcasting station, newspaper, or magazine may be operated?

7. Does a **regulating code** for the media exist? Is it

self-imposed and self-regulated? Are the codes actually followed?

8. Is the news media generally regarded to be credible? Do you agree? Is the foreign media regarded as more or less credible than the national media?

## C. Control of the Media

1. Who owns and controls the media within the country? Private groups, political parties, government, individuals?

2. To what extent does the ownership of the media appear to influence the media content?

3. How are the different forms of the media **financed**? How does the financing affect what is communicated?

4. What is the education, background, and sex of reporters and writers? Are they representative of the population? Does their background influence what and how they report information? Do newsmen seem to report the news objectively? If not, why not?

5. Do journalism and broadcasting schools exist within the country? If not, where do people in these fields get their training? What region and social class do the students come from?

## D. Access and Feedback

1. Is the media accessible to all of the people? What is the price of newspapers, magazines, radios, and televisions?

2. How does the media deal with **language differences** within the country? Are there groups that are not represented or addressed by the media?

3. Do the media forms allow for feedback from the audience or subscribers (letters to the editor, reply opportunities, complaints)?

4. If someone you know wished to air a complaint or publicize something and receive media coverage, how would he go about it? Through what channels must his message pass?

5. Can complaints from the public lead to license removal for a broadcasting station, newspaper, or magazine?

6. Is violence a possible means of obtaining media coverage? Could lack of coverage of problems of certain groups lead to violence? Has this occurred?

## E. Content

1. What percentage of content in the different media systems is devoted to the following categories:
   a. international news
   b. national news
   c. local news
   d. education
   e. public service
   f. local programming
   g. cultural events
   h. entertainment
   i. advertising

Are there requirements for such categories, especially in the broadcast media? On what basis is media content determined (ratings, subscriptions, government decree)?

2. Do you think a percentage increase in any of the categories would contribute to the welfare and development of the country? Which one(s)? Why?

3. To what extent are there **foreign** broadcasts, programming, films, newspapers, and magazines? Is there a quota on foreign programming and films? What are the positive and negative effects of this quota?

4. How does the press obtain its news concerning the government? If news conferences are held, are they open

and unrehearsed?

5. Is political advertising allowed through the media? Is it limited?

---

**We live in a fantastic century...
We hear on all sides that East and West
are meeting, but it is an understatement.
They are being flung at one another with
the force of atoms, the speed of jets,
the restlessness of minds impatient to
learn of ways that differ from their own.
From the perspective of history this may
prove to be the most important fact about
the twentieth century. When historians
look back upon our years they may
remember them...as the time in which
all the peoples of the world
first had to take one another seriously.**

**--Huston Smith**

---

## F. Orientation

1. How quickly is news disseminated? How soon after an event does the news reach you? From what source? In what form? What channels were passed before the news reached you?

2. What seems to be the basic **philosophy** or orientation of the press (authoritarianism, libertarianism, social responsibility, other)?

3. To what extent do newspapers, magazines, radio, and TV editorialize? Do some newspapers and broadcasting stations always take a pro-government stance?

4. Does the news media make an effort to investigate

and provide background information for news stories, in order to aid audience and readers in understanding the causes and significance of events?

## G. Media Habits

1. Do the media habits of adults differ from those of younger people?

2. Do the media habits of one class or group of people differ from others? Why?

3. Are viewing, listening, and reading usually done in groups (e.g. posted newspapers, large groups sitting around a single radio or TV set)? Where? Are the groups organized? Do they meet regularly?

4. Is information usually diffused by means of an *opinion leader* who follows the media and then discusses the information with others?

---

> **The power of the west--through economic, military, political, communication, and cultural structures--presently impedes rather than supports authentic development for most of the third world.**
>
> **--Richard Barnet**

---

5. Does the population look to the media primarily for education and information, or entertainment? Other things?

## H. Effects of the Media

1. Is the media changing the habits and daily routines of the people (e.g. more time spent at home, less socializing among neighbors, new patterns of consumption)?

2. What are the effects of the foreign media? What is its relative importance? What would be the effect of in-

creasing or decreasing the amount of foreign media?

3. Has the media created an international awareness that is leading to political action?

4. Is the media aiding or hindering the country's efforts at development? In what ways? How can media participation be more effective for development?

# Health and Welfare

Problems of nutrition
reflect the global situation;
one can substitute
the term 'underfed'
for 'underdeveloped,'
the term 'fed' or 'overfed'
for 'developed.'
—CERES

# Health and Welfare

## A. Nutrition

Obtain some basic agricultural data which deals with the food production for consumption within the country. Food balance sheets for the country would also help. If you are concentrating on one minority or one region of the country, be sure to make allowances. In addition, look at socioeconomic data on the marketing practices of the country, on the distribution of goods, and on the storage of crops. From this information, answer the following questions:

1. What are the basic **carbohydrate** foods in the people's diet? How are they prepared? How are they processed? Can you suggest ways to improve either procedure? Is the crop raised by the family for family consumption or for export? Can you think of ways in which the carbohydrate production could be improved and better distributed? What percentage of family income and/or work energy goes into getting the basic carbohydrate foods? Compare this to your experience in your native country.

2. What are the basic **protein** sources? How much does it cost relative to carbohydrate sources? In terms of its amino acid composition, how *good* is it as protein? How much is consumed per week? Where does the protein come from? How is it processed and prepared? What percentage of the people can afford an adequate protein source? How might the percentage be raised? How is protein food distributed among the members of a family at any given meal?

3. Obtain data sheets which indicate daily **vitamin and mineral** requirements and vitamin and mineral composition of various foods. If basic foods of the area are not

included, try to find out their nutrient content from local health personnel. Given the foods eaten, does it appear that an average individual is receiving adequate quantities of vitamins and minerals? How does the processing and preparation of food affect nutrient content?

4. What are the basic sources of **fat** in the diet? What is the fat/protein ratio?

5. Nationally, is there a **cash crop** program which undermines the nutritional level of the population? Why does the government encourage this? What kind of crops or food products are not distributed adequately within the country?

6. What is the role of the **sea** in the food production of the country? What are the dangers involved in commercial fishing as far as depleting the supply is concerned? Is life better by the sea than inland? Why?

7. How does the government combat malnutrition? Advertising? International groups who operate nutrition clinics? Importation of grain? How effective are its measures? What will it do in times of food shortage?

8. Follow the path of one crop from a small farm through the various middlemen until it reaches the consumer. What does your path say about the effective distribution of food products within the country? Are some products just priced out of reach of the lower classes? Who controls the distribution system? Relate this to corruption and political influence.

9. Take a look at the **foreign companies** which deal in foodstuffs. What kind of approach do they take in selling their products? Is their approach educational or emotional? Do they encourage the consumption of nutritionally poor foods? Do they play upon the attractions of packaging rather than content to persuade the local populace to substitute the foreign product for a local product? If no direct substitution is made (e.g. canned milk in the place of fresh goat's milk), then what

products are not purchased because of the consumption of foreign foods (e.g. Coke in the place of rice)? Estimate the waste generated when cash from local crop sales is exchanged for foreign goods. Compare the prices of American goods in the country with those you have seen at home; compare them with prices of comparable local goods.

10. Try to discern some **food consumption patterns** within the family group, within the community, and within the nation as a whole. Does the average person appear to be well-fed and healthy? Which individuals (e.g. women in the family), and which groups (e.g. urban poor) have the lowest nutritional status? How long do mothers breast-feed their children? What happens after weaning? Are there food taboos associated with the culture or with any groups within the country which might affect the nutritional status? Investigate the traditional foods of the country for nutritional effect.

11. Make a dietary survey of the food consumption of a group of people. Analyze it for nutritional content.

12. Look at the **vital statistics** of the community or country. What are the mortality rates for infants? What does this say about nutritional concerns? Investigate morbidity patterns of the country or community. What does this say about the nutritional levels of the areas with a greater prevalence of disease?

13. If you can, perform **anthropometric studies** to determine the physical development patterns of children. Relate any findings which appear abnormal to possible nutritional deficiencies.

14. If you can get access to clinical records, study the record of physical signs which the doctor may list with his diagnosis. Relate things like prevalence of skin diseases, malfunctioning nerves or malformed bones, and general fatigue to what you know about nutrition.

## B. Water Supply

1. How pure is the water supply? How expensive is bottled water? What kind of precautionary measures are taken to insure an adequately clean supply of water? Does the weather affect its purity?

2. How are wastes disposed of? How are garbage and refuse disposed of? Is there a sewage system? How efficient is it? Can you relate the method of waste disposal to any diseases which are prevalent? How does the government help in this problem?

3. What substitutes are there for water? What do children drink? Is this good for them?

## C. Health Care Delivery

1. Visit local health care facilities. Try to establish a gradation in your mind, from district dispensaries (primary centers) to health centers (secondary centers) to hospitals (tertiary centers). Obtain information from the national health office about the overall organization and distribution of health care facilities, procedures for training health personnnel and staffing health centers, and for mechanisms of insurance and payment. Is health care based on a preventive or a curative model? Are psychological factors considered important? Get an idea of the spectrum and number of health care workers in your area: folk curers, midwives, paramedics, nurses, public health workers, lab and x-ray technicians, dentists and doctors. Meet with some of these people and discuss with them their work, their lives, and their relationships with other community members.

2. Describe a **district dispensary**. How are they financed? Are they government, missionary, or privately controlled? Who works there? How many workers? How are they trained? What is the division of labor? What is the degree of responsibility of non-M.D.s? What spectrum of illnesses can they diagnose and treat?

3. Describe a **community health center** in a similar fashion. In addition, is there a lab? X-ray unit? Dental unit? Minor surgical equipment? A set-up for IV infusion? Beds for overnight stays? Emergency equipment?

4. Describe a **hospital** in a similar fashion. What is the availability of specialists? How many beds are there? For what illnesses are patients hospitalized? For how long? How is their hospitalization financed? How are they fed? Can the family live-in?

5. Visit other kinds of institutions: mental hospitals, tuberculosis sanitoriums, leper colonies. Try to understand the general process whereby a person is identified as *ill*, physically or mentally, and placed in an institution. Try to meet some patients and see how they feel. Talk with their families and see how *they* feel.

6. In each type of health care facility, describe the **patient population.** How many patient visits are allowed or take place each day? Are there seasonal fluctuations, daily fluctuations (e.g. market days)? Describe the scene in the waiting room. Is it a long wait? Who in the community uses the facility? Who doesn't and why? Describe the administrative and medical procedure of processing a typical patient. Is the place personable or cold? Do the people seem enthusiastic, indifferent, or afraid?

7. Is a clinic visit or hospitalization expensive? Are drugs expensive, and if so, are they purchased? Who pays? Do the rates charged for any of these services reflect costs? Are they subsidized? Are they on a sliding-scale, to reflect the patient's ability to pay? Does the government set maximum rates? Do doctors simply charge what they wish? What forms of payment are acceptable? Is anyone denied treatment, if unable to pay?

8. Meet and talk with non-professional health personnel (e.g. folk curers and midwives). How do they relate to the professional health care system? How does the

system (the professional workers) relate to them? Who in the community goes to non-professionals for help? Are there illnesses that the people think that the professional system can't deal with? That folk curers can't deal with? What kinds of taboos are there concerning professional health care? Can you see ways in which the two systems can beneficially interrelate? In what ways have the two systems already affected each other?

9. What **health education** programs exist? Describe them. Who do they affect? Do they seem to be effective? What programs in public health and preventive medicine exist? Do they seem to be effective? How do people react to vaccination programs?

## D. Disease Patterns (Western Conception)

These questions are directed towards an understanding of what diseases are prevalent, and how they affect social structure.

1. Obtain information from the national department of health on **mortality and morbidity** statistics, and statistics on disease incidence and prevalence. Allow a 3-5 year span for vital statistics, so as to avoid an atypical year. (Remember that sickness rates are poorly recorded even in the U.S. The highest-rate areas may simply be those with the best systems of detection and treatment.) What are the major diseases of the region and the nation?

2. What are the major **infectious** diseases? Pneumonia? Measles? Whooping cough? Tuberculosis? Middle ear infection? Colds? Tetanus? Diptheria? Polio? Typhoid? Smallpox? Chickenpox? Venereal diseases? Cholera? What is the approximate mortality rate by age from these diseases? How do the people view the nature of these diseases? Do they understand the concept *contagious*? Have immunization programs been instituted? Describe them. How are these programs regarded? What different modes of treatment are used by western-trained personnel and folk-curers? How successful are each?

3. What are the major **parasitic** diseases? Malaria? Amoebiasis? Worm infection (e.g. ascaris, hookworm)? Trichinosis? Schistosomiasis? What is the route of transmission of these organisms? What steps are taken to control their spread? Does the government have DDT spray programs against mosquitoes? Are they effective? How does DDT affect the ecology of the area?

4. What are the basic **nutritional** diseases? What specific vitamin and mineral deficiencies occur (e.g. iron deficiency/anemia, iodine deficiency/goiter, calcium deficiency/rickets)? Is the major protein source deficient in any essential amino acids? Are marasmus (starvation--primarily an urban problem) and kwashiorkor (protein malnutrition--primarily a rural problem) present?

5. What are the medical problems of the **pregnant woman** and the newborn child? What is the diet of the pregant woman? Who advises her on this diet? What is the incidence of toxemia of pregnancy? What is the incidence of spontaneous abortion? What percentage of births take place outside of hospitals and clinics? Who performs them? What is the nature of the midwifery system? Do midwives use sterile technique? Is there neonatal tetanus and sepsis? What are the breast-feeding practices of the women? When is the child usually weaned? What is the child fed after weaning? What is the approximate mortality rate at birth? Year 1? Year 2? Are there many congenital defects? What means exist for correction of these defects?

6. Is diarrhea and subsequent dehydration of the weanling a serious problem? Think about how the people get diarrhea, how they deal with the problem, and how it might ideally be solved. Think about the ecological flow of pathogens through the environment. Do the people understand the concept of a *microorganism*? What is the approximate mortality rate from dehydration? How do people react when you suggest they boil their water?

7. What other major diseases are there? Heart disease? Bronchitis? Emphysema? Diabetes? Asthma? Hypertension? Cancer? Menopausal problems? Trauma (e.g. cuts, bullet wounds)? Genito-urinary infections? Ulcers? Constipation? Skin infections? Arthritis? Dental problems? Is there need for general surgery?

## E. Folk Medicine

1. Is there a strong tradition of folk medicine? Who are the healers? How are they selected and trained? What kinds of remedies, cures, and potions are prepared and used by the folk-curers?

2. Describe some typical healing scenes.

3. How often is the supernatural invoked to explain physical ailments? Who is called upon and what is used to cure people of this kind of problem? Is any folk medicine practiced by the lay individual?

4. How effective is folk medicine? How much is folk medicine used? What elements of the population depend on it wholly? In part? Not at all?

5. What criteria does a person use in deciding whether to rely on folk or western medicine?

## F. Effects of Illness on Social Structure

1. How does disease affect the community or nation (e.g. epidemics)? Obtain statistics on recent epidemics.

2. Visit a household with a sick person. What is the nature of the inter-personal dynamics in such a household? Who cares for the sick person? What special privileges does the sick person have? How is *falling ill* viewed in the culture (bad luck, evil, neutral)? Do there seem to be *roles* that individuals of different ages and sexes play when stricken with a given illness? Who takes on the normal work of the sick person? How do relatives and/or neighbors respond? How do various individuals (mother, brother, godfather, neighbor, etc.) and/or the collective community respond to the illness of a newborn

baby, a young child, a pregnant woman, a working man, an elder woman or man, a village leader, a member of a different race or religion?

3. Make similar observations on a household and a community on the occasion of a birth and a death. What are some of the midwives' rituals? What beliefs exist concerning treatment of the baby? Diet of the mother? How do various individuals respond to a death? Describe a funeral. How do individuals pay homage to the dead?

4. How are the physically-handicapped treated? What kinds of aids are available to them?

## G. Social, Legal, and Political Aspects of Health Care

1. What is the difference between the level of health care available to the rich, and that available to most people?

2. Are there laws governing the sale of **drugs**? Who produces these drugs? How do prices compare with U.S. prices? Who can afford to buy drugs?

3. Do a high percentage of medical school graduates leave the country to practice? Where do they go? Why? If they go to the developed countries, is it because the developed countries need them? Why is this true?

4. Do any regulations exist to prevent the loss of medical personnel through emigration? Are these regulations being effectively enforced?

5. Does the government conceal epidemics, instances of famine, or other health problems, for political or economic reasons (e.g. potential threat to the tourist industry)? How does this affect potential aid from international relief organizations? How does this affect the people involved?

## H. Family Planning

1. Describe the family planning program in this country.

What are its goals? Who funds it? Why? Is family planning an official government policy? Do government or private organizations predominate?

2. What methods are used to further planned parenthood? How successful are they?

3. What kinds of **traditional beliefs** or practices make it difficult to convince women of the benefits of spacing births? To convince men? Which sex is considered responsible for birth control?

4. The disadvantages of high population growth are usually stressed--but what **economic factors** make large families advantageous? For parents, does security in old age depend upon having large numbers of children?

5. What are some of the other factors leading to underdevelopment that can explain poverty more completely than rapid population growth? How might some of these factors be changed, and who has the power to do so?

6. What percentage of the sexually-active population is using a contraceptive? Which is the most popular? Why?

7. How expensive are clinic visits, IUD insertions, pills, and other contraceptives? Does the use of any of these involve a significant economic sacrifice?

8. What is the future of family planning in your native country? Does your country need to control its population? If so, why? How urgently is this needed? It has been suggested that it is not the *size* of the population that is most significant, but rather the *wastefulness* of the consumption model the society follows. What do you think?

## I. Ecological Considerations

1. What types of **pollution** can you identify? Noise, air, water pollution? How are they caused? Is there anything being done to correct them? What role does the government take? What role do students play? What is the future of the environment of this country? Can you

balance the costs of environmental deterioration against the costs of underdevelopment? Is there any way to develop and yet maintain the environment? How conscious are foreign firms regarding pollution of the local environment? Is there clear-cutting or strip-mining being carried out by foreign firms? Why is this allowed?

2. Are lands over-worked to the point of erosion and depletion? Are seas yielding as much as they used to yield to the fishermen? What are the effects of new methods of agriculture upon the ecological system? What are the effects of new methods of fishing? What is the future of the crop lands and of the seas of this country?

## J. Housing

1. What is the local concept of a house, and its primary **functions**?

2. How do present housing **conditions** meet these criteria?

3. Is there enough housing? How many people live in an average house? In how many rooms? Is the housing adequate for healthy living? If conditions are very cramped, what is the effect on the social relations of the family or group members involved?

4. Do the people need to **heat** their homes for part of the year? How do they do so?

5. Given the cultural/climatic context, are there any additional functions you feel housing in this nation should serve? Why?

6. Are houses located close together? How is their location determined?

7. What **materials** are used in house construction? Are they available locally?

8. What methods of construction are used?

9. Do people build their own houses? Do they work in

groups on each other's houses?

10. How expensive is housing?

11. What is the **government's role** in housing its citizens?

12. Are there any particular aspects of the local housing that you would like to incorporate into your own housing in the future?

## K. Clothing

1. How expensive is clothing? Is it generally durable and long-lasting? How are clothes cleaned?

2. Are clothes or cloth material imported, or brought in from another region? How has this affected the local cloth industry?

3. Do some people make their own garments? What kind of equipment do they use?

4. Are clothing styles always traditional? If not, who are the style-setters?

5. Are many people without adequate clothing for the climate? What kinds of problems arise due to inadequate clothing?

## L. Worker's Safety

1. Are there any government or company regulations regarding work safety practices? How carefully are these followed? Compare foreign firms to local firms.

2. How long is a normal work day? In agriculture, transportation, local marketing, retail trade, local crafts, mining, and manufacturing? Do foreign enterprises differ from these patterns? Are there child-labor laws? Laws governing the employment of women? In which sectors? How necessary is it for men, women, and children to work regardless of the conditions?

3. What kinds of industrial accidents occur? What is the incidence? How might they be prevented? Will they be prevented?

# The
# Trans-
# Cultural
# Experience

He who travels far will often see things
far from what he believed was truth...
—Hermann Hesse

# The Trans-Cultural Experience

## A. Personal Awareness and Growth

1. Albert Camus writes: *Your successes and happiness are forgiven you only if you generously consent to share them. But to be happy it is essential not to be too concerned with others. Consequently, there is no escape. Happy and judged, or absolved and wretched.*

If you have been confronted with a very impoverished situation and witnessed more suffering than ever before in your life, have you had this sense that your own happiness is incompatible with a deep concern for others? How can you deal with it? To what extent does guilt influence or motivate you?

2. Levi-Strauss writes: *Why does he (the anthropologist) decide to disdain (his own society), reserving for societies distant and different from his own the patience and devotion which he has deliberately withheld from his fellow-citizens?...At home the anthropologist may be a natural subversive, a convinced opponent of traditional usage; but no sooner has he in focus a society different from his own than he becomes respectful of even the most conservative practices.*

Have you found that at times, out of a desire to be respectful of your host culture, you have been unnaturally conservative about social forms? If you are in some ways an advocate of a counter-culture in your own country, do you see any inconsistency between your actions here and there? If so, why do you think this is true? Should you be more tolerant and patient with your own society? On the other hand, societies are living, changing entities. They depend upon the actions and thinking of their members for energy and new directions. Would you agree that behavior differing radically from social norms is acceptable for a native of a particular society? Would the same behavior on the part of a foreigner be unacceptable? Discuss.

3. Have you found a lack of the kind of intellectual orientation and discussion which you are familiar with in a university environment? Why? Would this happen at home if you were away from the university? What concerns occupy the local people--meditation, art, complicated games, other? If you have experienced intellectual and/or emotional solitude, have you been able to use this to work within yourself? In what ways?

4. To what extent have you found yourself to be self-directed and self-motivated intellectually? In all your other activities? How would you compare your present work and its vitality with that which you usually experience within the university?

5. Do you feel that thoroughgoing **communication** with your local friends is very difficult, because you don't have similar life experiences? What new modes of communication have you developed?

6. In what ways are your personal habits of **consumption** and spending changing? Do you find yourself more meticulous about your possessions and more thrifty with your money? Why? How do you think this will affect you when you return to your native country? Why? If you don't think the two are related, why not?

7. How have your thoughts about further academic work and potential career been influenced by your experience in this country?

8. What has your experience told you about the notion of boundaries of race, culture, and nation among peoples of the world? How has your ability to penetrate another society and culture affected the above? Is the term *boundaries* appropriate? What would be a better term?

9. In terms of reinterpreting and modifying your life-style, do you think that you have adopted many practices and ideas from the culture you are in? What kinds?

10. In what ways have you found yourself to be clearly a product of your own culture in your habits, orientations, expectations, motives, and mind-frame? What specific aspects of yourself are *cultural baggage*, and which are essential to your personal identity (e.g. whereas a lack of concern about time and punctuality may cause trouble for you in our culture, in others in may be expected and reinforced)? To what extent can you conform to local values and expectations and still be yourself? Consider your social behavior, personal experience, mannerisms, and habits in the cross-cultural setting.

---

**Reporter to Gandhi:   'What do you think of western civilization?'**

**Gandhi to Reporter:   'I think it would be a good idea.'**

---

11. What is necessary for you to be happy and fulfilled in your everyday life? To what extent may these needs be met in the new cultural setting (e.g. privacy, intimate companionship, honest feedback, intellectual stimulation/communication of a particular kind, certain favorite foods)? Do you think you will find yourself *caught in between* two cultures? How do you think your experience will make it difficult to live in your native country?

12. *Culture shock* has been defined as *the need for something familiar* and *excessive irritation from minor frustrations*. Describe this phenomenon in relation to your own experience. What differences seem most noticeable initially? After a period of time in your new environment? How would **you** define *culture shock*?

## B. Interactions

1. *Cultural fatigue* has been defined as *the lack of energy or emotional projection for social relations.* Discuss this in relation to your own experiences, pointing out possible ways to resolve the problem of *cultural fatigue.*

2. Describe your experiences of **miscommunication** when talking or making plans with local people (e.g. perhaps when your friend says *yes* he actually means *maybe,* and when he says *maybe,* he is trying to imply *no*).

3. **Body language** provides cues in situations where thoughts and feelings are not expressed verbally. However, there is much room for misunderstanding this type of communication in cross-cultural relations. Consider the example of relations with the opposite sex, where eye contact, a smile, and hand-holding may communicate something entirely different than what you are accustomed to. Consider how non-verbal communication operates to express the following: romantic interest, anger in varying degrees (withdrawal, violence, or excessive politeness?), impatience, boredom, sadness, happiness, maturity, authority, respect, and shame.

---

**To feel vulnerable--that is, to feel cheated yet powerless next to the literate, the well-fed, and the well-employed--is to begin to understand a feeling common in poor countries. Whole societies, not just individuals, may feel vulnerable.**

**--Denis Goulet**

---

4. Consider **your role** in the community, as a teacher or student, and as a foreigner representing certain values and ideals. What influence might these have on the local people?

5. What do the local people think are the most salient characteristics of your own culture? This may lead to some additional insight into their self-image as well.

6. What impact has the local community and the teaching or studying experience had on your own values, ideals, and views of the world?

## C. Sense of Humor

1. What kinds of humor are acceptable? What forms do they take? Are practical jokes common?

---

**Laughter and joy
are nourishments
upon which
any human endeavor thrives.**

---

2. Are there any topical areas that are taboo or given special emphasis (e.g. government activity, sex, corruption)?

3. What seem to be the elements of a good joke?

4. What kinds of jokes are told about foreigners?

5. Do these people commonly laugh at themselves? Are they inclined to laugh at their difficulties?

6. Is odd behavior met with ridicule, or amusement?

7. Do the people find foreign accents or ways amusing?

8. What kind of humor predominates in films? TV? Radio?

9. Are jokes ever shared between individuals of different status? Is a person likely to tell a joke to a superior?

---

**The most important piece of luggage
is and remains a joyful heart.**

**--Hermann Lons**

---

# Development

No one is being developed:
one develops oneself.

--CERES

# Development

Until recent years, much of the discussion of *development* centered around economics. No longer is that enough of a concern. Most observers of the world scene now admit that meaningful development must be broadly defined to encompass a great many other things. Such a definition means that development issues are woven through all of the other chapters of this book.

## A. General Questions

One way in which *development* can be approached is to ask the following questions:

1. What is the nature of *underdevelopment*? What do local people stress? What does the foreign community stress?

2. What are the goals of development? Who has formulated these goals? Who is participating in this effort? What do the common people think of the government's goals for development? Do they have a sense of active involvement and participation in development? Is development something that will happen *for* them or *with* them, as they understand it? Or *for* someone else, and not them?

3. What institutions, structures, and relationships create or contribute to the perpetuation of *underdevelopment*? What is the origin and history of these institutions, structures, and relationships? How many of these involve foreigners?

4. To what extent does this country control its own resources, both human and natural? Could this be used as a measure of *underdevelopment*?

5. What institutions, structures, and relationships help to break through the obstacles to development? What

created and propells these?

6. What is the role of ideas in development? What is the role of concrete action? What interaction exists between the two?

7. Does *development* as defined by the elite include anything for the masses of people?

8. What can be ecologically-sound development? Has there been an influx of high-polluting foreign industry? What trade-offs do the local people see as reasonable between environmental standards and development goals?

---

**Consider these two schools of 'development education':**

**Charity--**
**They are the problem.**
**We help the victims.**
**Give a little more.**
**Generosity is the answer.**

**Redistribution--**
**We are the problem.**
**We create the victims.**
**Take a little less.**
**Changes in structures and lifestyles is the answer.**

**--Jorgen Lissner**

---

9. What could be sound development from a religious and cultural point of view? What is the attitude of the elites and the common people towards foreign values? Towards preservation of local cultural identity? Is there a concerted effort on the part of the government to instill a

new national identity upon its people? What is the reaction of the people?

10. What is the nature of the *developed* countries? In what ways can they be said to be *underdeveloped*? In what ways can they be said to be *overdeveloped*? Do the industrial and social patterns of the developed countries include an internal stability and a balance with nature? If not, are they a useful pattern to follow?

11. What problems do the local scientists address themselves to? How relevant are these endeavors to the daily problems that face the population?

12. How appropriate is the capital/labor mix of modern technology to the availability of each within the country? (See the questions on *foreign investment* in the section on *ECONOMICS*.)

13. What are the implications of the findings of the Club of Rome--that the world could not support its current population at the standard of living of Americans in 1970?

14. *In 1964-65, some 11,000 interns and residents in American hospitals—out of a total of 41,000—were graduates of foreign medical schools, and more than 8,000 of them came from low-income countries.*

—**Tibor Mende**

How does the *brain drain* manifest itself in this country? Is the government doing anything to attempt to stop this loss of manpower? Are such attempts successful?

15. What advantages and disadvantages derive from the extended family? How does the position of old people in your native country differ with that in this country? What effects is *development* having on the extended family as an institution?

16. How does tourism figure in government planning for development? What effects does tourism have on the availability of foreign exchange, lives of artists of all

kinds, lives of young people, and lives of the peasants?

17. Are the cities overcrowded? Why do people move to the cities? Are there any government attempts to bring industry to the rural areas?

18. Is population control a prerequisite for development, or is development itself a pre-requisite for population control? (The first position assumes that more people must divide a fixed quantity of goods and services. The second suggests that more hands can produce more goods and services—a perspective which gives the villager an important economic incentive to have many children.)

---

**We must distinguish between 'cultural obstacles to development' and what Gunnar Myrdal calls 'the frustrating effects of poverty.'**

**—Michael Cangiani**

---

## B. Reflections

The following quotations merit thoughtful comments:

1. *For the larger part of the labor force in under-developed countries, we must discard entirely the concept of 'unemployment' and 'underemployment' as inadequate to reality. We have to base our analysis of labor utilization on simple behavioral concepts: which people work at all; for what periods during the day, week, month, and year do they work; and with what intensity and effectiveness.*

**—Gunnar Myrdal**

2. *Development towards what?*

3. *...growth must come out of our own roots, not*

*through the grafting on to those of something which is alien to our society.*

—**Julius Nyerere**

---

**A fullness of good and the abundance of goods are not synonymous: a person may have much and be mediocre or have little and be rich. Nevertheless, persons need to have a certain quantity of goods in order to be fully human.**

—**Denis Goulet**

---

4. *How does a society treat its old people, and indeed, all its members who are not useful and productive in the narrowest sense? Judged by this standard, the so-called advanced societies have a lot to learn which the so-called backward societies could teach them...*

—**Dr. K. Kaunda**
President, Rep. of Zambia

5. *The eagerness with which the elites of the emergent nations seize the pre-packed solutions propounded, is a tribute to the efficiency of the educational processing to which these groups have been subjected by the White North, and an index of the gap between them and the largely peasant, largely collective societies whose interests they are supposed to represent.*

—**Prof. Keith Buchanan**
University of Sydney

6. *In 8 years, Brazil nearly doubled coffee production, but earnings fell by 35%.*

*In 1963 Tanzania needed to produce 5 tons of sisal to buy a tractor. In 1970 it had to produce 10 tons of sisal to buy that same tractor.*

*In 1950 exports from poorer nations were 30% of the world total; by 1970 they were less than 18%.*

7. *The era of low-cost energy is almost dead. Popey is running out of spinach.*

**—U.S. Secretary of Commerce**

8. *The choice of technology is one of the most important decisions that a country can make.*

Important questions that bear directly on the topic of *development* are to be found also in the sections on *SOCIAL STRUCTURE*, *HEALTH*, *COMMUNICA—TIONS*, *EDUCATION*, *POLITICS*, and particularly *ECONOMICS*.

## The VIA Health Handbook

This guide to health maintenance has been used by VIA volunteers for several years. It includes brief summaries of the major tropical diseases, parasites, and other health problems, and describes the symptoms of each for early identification. Pocket-size copies in booklet form are available for one dollar from Volunteers in Asia, Box 4543, Stanford, California, 64305.